The
Book of CRYSTAL
HEALING

The
Book of # CRYSTAL
HEALING

LIZ SIMPSON

Gaia Books Limited

A GAIA ORIGINAL

*Books from Gaia celebrate the vision of
Gaia, the self-sustaining living Earth,
and seek to help its readers live in
greater personal and planetary harmony.*

Editorial	Jo Godfrey Wood
	Clare Stewart
Design	Sara Mathews
Illustration	Mark Preston
Photography	Adrian Swift
Production	Lyn Kirby
Managing editor	Pip Morgan
Direction	Patrick Nugent
Consultants	Ruth White, healer
	Cathy Oldershaw, gemmologist

® This is a Registered Trade Mark of Gaia Books Limited

Copyright © 1997 Gaia Books Limited, London
Text Copyright © 1997 by Liz Simpson

First published in the United Kingdom in 1997 by
Gaia Books Ltd, 66 Charlotte St, London W1P 1LR
and 20 High St, Stroud, Glos GL5 1AS

Internet: www.gaiabook.co.uk

ISBN 1-85675-029-9

A catalogue record of this book is available from the British Library.

Printed and bound by Dai Nippon, Hong Kong

10 9 8 7 6 5 4 3 2

A NOTE FROM THE AUTHOR

The following is an explanation of crystal healing which pulls together all the concepts this book raises. Refer to it constantly as you work through Chapters Three to Five.

Crystal healing works on the principle that every cell in the body vibrates at its own specific frequency. When these natural frequencies become unbalanced, we experience dis-ease. Crystals oscillate to a natural healing frequency that is activated by mental energy. Powered by strong intention – either your own or that of your therapist – healing energy is channelled through the crystal from an inexplicable source, often referred to as the Universal Life Force. The appropriate healing energy – stimulating, balancing, or tranquillizing – is transmitted from the Universal Life Force and amplified through the unique molecular structure of natural crystals. This helps to harmonize and balance the body's frequencies back to optimum, healthy levels.

Working with crystals is an intuitive process. Through the meditations and guided visualizations outlined in this book, you will be able to tap into your inherent self-healing abilities. Crystals are merely one form of healing tool, or catalyst, that directs that ability in a particularly powerful way.

CONTENTS

◆

CLEAR QUARTZ PYRAMID

◆

FOREWORD

◆

Our planet is rich with the beauty of crystals – from the diamond which they tell us is "forever" to the silicon chip that stores information never dreamed possible fifty years ago. Anthropologists have unearthed mysterious artefacts such as crystal skulls so precisely fashioned that even today's high-tech instruments are incapable of duplicating them. Then they speculate: Were these splendid forms of sculpted light carved over generations by women who polished each curve and shaped each plane with their hair, or were they a gift to us from extra-terrestrials designed to carry information and spiritual energies capable of changing our lives, if only we could penetrate their mysteries?

New Age healers, resurrecting ancient practices, reach for emeralds, sapphires, topaz, aquamarines, and jade, directing their energies towards different chakras – the body's spinning energy vortices which are believed to control our physical and spiritual well-being – in an attempt to shift life energy, or Qi, and re-establish balance, harmony, and better health.

The world of crystals is vast and glorious. But it can also be enormously confusing. Walk into any New Age book shop and you will find any number of books on the subject of crystals and their use. Some purport to be "channelled" material: others have a more scientific bent. Most are filled with conflicting information that leads to more confusion than clarity when, in an attempt to penetrate the mysteries of crystals and find out how to make some practical use of them, you riffle through their pages.

Not so *The Book of Crystal Healing*. Liz Simpson has created a unique source of beauty, information, and inspiration for the crystal-curious like myself. This book takes you through the history of gemstones and quartz crystals, examining their use as weapons and tools, as objects of divination, in jewellery, and as talismans and amulets. It looks at the specific healing properties of precious and semi-precious stones and then gives you more than a glimpse of the fascinating high-tech world of the science behind these enigmas of Nature in a simple and thoroughly comprehensible way. It looks at their formation, their energy-carrying properties, the electromagnetic influences they exert on our lives and how they too can be influenced through thought and energy.

Perhaps most valuable of all, here you will find a wealth of encouraging information, inspiration and advice for anyone wanting to begin to develop his or her own relationship to crystals and gemstones. Ancient Shamanic traditions hold that the relationship between a crystal of any sort and the person using it is highly individual. This relationship, shamans insist, is best developed by journeying into non-ordinary reality and meeting with the Great Crystal from whom each of us individually can learn how best to work with crystal energies to enhance our own lives – and even more important – the lives and health of others. Here in this beautiful book you will find much inspiration for making that journey.

Leslie Kenton

INTRODUCTION

$\diamond$

"The most beautiful thing we can experience is the mysterious.
Recognition of the mystery of the universe
is the course of all true Science."

ALBERT EINSTEIN (1879-1955)

The answer to the question "what is a crystal?" depends very much on to whom you direct it. To a geologist crystals of all shapes, sizes, and chemical compositions reveal astounding atomic symmetry. The molecules which form the new layers of a growing crystal stack themselves on top of the previous matrix in identical, ordered units. A jeweller would tell you that the most desirable crystals are called gemstones. Because of their beauty and hardness they are used to make decorative items, often with a high price tag.

To an historian, crystals are a means of interpreting our cultural heritage. Finds from the graves of royalty as well as artefacts unearthed from ancient dwellings reveal the changing desirability of gemstones since antiquity. Someone working within industry might point out ways in which crystalline material plays a vital role in technology – from diamond-tipped drills to the synthetic silicon chips in computers. And a complementary health therapist would say that a crystal is a tool with which individuals can direct, focus, and amplify healing energy. All these areas are addressed in the following pages, but we are mainly concerned with crystal healing.

The notion that a crystal, regarded by many as nothing more than a pretty stone, can directly benefit our health may at first appear rather weird or "New Age". In some cases that is perfectly understandable, given the flaky metaphysics used to explain it by some crystal "experts". Orthodox science lends weight to the belief that crystal healing has no validity by refusing to try to explain it. Crystal healing does not fit current scientific principles, therefore it must be false. Neither of these views is accurate or acceptable. What this book aims to do is to steer a path between the rigidity of scientific materialism and the woolliness of New Age notions.

It has taken us 4000 years to scientifically validate what ancient wisdom teaches. That there is a force in nature, invisible and imperceptible to most of modern humankind, which plays a vital role in health and healing. This force has been called many things – Universal Life Force, "chi", pure Consciousness, prana, the Universal Field. Regardless of what you choose to call it (in this book it is called the Universal Life Force) this inexplicable source of life courses through all things and in doing so produces an outer energy field referred to as the "aura". This is often depicted as halos surrounding the bodies of holy people in religious paintings spanning many centuries and all continents. What may surprise you is that you also have an aura. And it is this which allows you to interact on a non-physical level with all things.

We now know that what underpins biochemistry is electromagnetism, a form of energy. It has taken quantum physics to show that what we perceive as solid matter is actually 99.9999% empty space filled with energy. By understanding that all matter is energy it is easier to understand how man can interact with crystal.

The next aspect of crystal healing to embrace is the fact that everything in the universe vibrates, albeit at different frequencies. We all have personal experience of this. We "pick up vibes" from some people, and say that those we don't get on with are "not on our wavelength".

Many doctors attracted to the burgeoning field of mind-body medicine accept that thoughts and emotions – forms of mental energy – play a signficant part in wellbeing. We can influence the state of our physical body beneficially or otherwise by what goes on in our mind. One of the words that you will come across constantly in Chapters Three to Five of this book is "intention". It is your thought energy that activates crystals. Your own strength of will helps direct, focus, and amplify the healing power of the Universal Life Force to stabilize the energies within your body. Our natural state is one of moving toward balance. Once our energy is brought into balance we experience optimum health.

We are all unique. No single therapy is suitable for everyone and crystal healing is no exception. Not everyone can spend the time, effort, mental concentration, and expense of working with full crystal layouts. With that in mind this book approaches the practice of crystal healing from three different – but equally beneficial – levels. You are simply asked to choose the one most relevant to you.

Firstly, there is the aesthetic appeal of crystals. Scientists are already aware that colour, shape, and texture each have distinct physiological effects. The positive emotions and feelings we get from appreciating beautiful things infuses us with a beneficial energy that helps bring our bodies and minds into balance. The first three chapters will give you a fuller appreciation of the remarkable properties of crystals.

Secondly, crystals are a metaphor for perfect order and balance because of their unique symmetrical structure. Hence they are a particularly apt meditative tool for general personal development as well as for balancing the human energy system. A full explanation of how to use crystals for meditation and visualization is found in Chapter Four.

Finally, Chapter Five outlines how crystals can be used as a viable physical tool for self-healing. A variety of simple crystal layouts for everyday concerns are offered.

For centuries man has revered crystals, not just for their beauty and economic value, but as healing tools. Gradually we are learning that ancient knowledge, once considered to be fanciful myth, is based on more than a grain of truth. Some scientists now postulate that inorganic, self-replicating crystals of clay were the template from which complex, organic molecules such as RNA and DNA formed. What we have done in three hundred years of mechanistic science is to wantonly disregard anything that doesn't fit with a model that only partially explains human existence. Thankfully, what was once considered "esoteric" – that is, secret or mysterious – is gradually finding acceptance among a new generation of scientists who realize that the human experience cannot be explained by scientific proof alone.

The following chapters contain everything you need for crystal healing. Except for one thing. When you buy certain products nowadays there is usually a sign on the box saying "batteries not included". With this book the only thing missing is your open mind.

1
CRYSTAL WORLDS

◆

"...there is an important and potentially very happy marriage between the spiritual, the mystical and scientific world views, because they are all methods for looking at the nature of reality."

ELIZABETH RAUSCHER, THE POWER OF PLACE

Imagine the wonderment of primitive man or woman stumbling across a uniquely shaped, brilliantly coloured, crystal among a vast expanse of amorphous, grey rock. Would it be any surprise if that person attributed mystical powers to it? Fundamental human instinct is for survival and to avoid trouble, from which spring countless taboos and superstitions. Many minerals have served to protect and appease spirits throughout history and have been made into talismans.

Historically, crystals have underpinned human development economically, technologically, and culturally. The importance of crystals links all civilizations across space and time. Until the current age of credit and "hidden assets", crystals were portable forms of wealth and status. We continue to construct roads and buildings using crystalline material such as granite and marble; concrete's rigidity and quick-setting properties depend on crystal growth. And cultures as far back as predynastic Egypt have used jewellery to celebrate human individuality.

Crystals help us to interpret the past. They teach us many things about humankind's cultural heritage. Their desirability in antiquity helps us to trace trading routes between far-flung civilizations. We can monitor changing fashions for gem material for decorative as well as medical purposes. Bound up with myth and magic, crystals help bring to light the different historical world views that have arisen down the ages concerning the immutable link between humans and nature.

CRYSTALS THROUGH THE AGES

TOOLS AND WEAPONS

Minerals were one of the catalysts that directed prehistoric people towards civilization. Either by accident or experiment their discovery of a property of quartz called "conchoidal fracture" led them to fashion tools and weapons instead of simply finding suitable material by chance. When two pieces of flint are struck together they may fracture and produce a curved, shell-like edge as sharp and effective as steel. Flint also exhibits a characteristic property known as piezoelectricity (see also p.42). When mechanical pressure is applied to certain crystals a static charge is produced that generates a spark with which to make fire. The same principle is utilized today in cigarette lighters. Several millennia after discovering the use of fire to heat, protect, and arm, humans used the effects of piezoelectricity in weapons of mass destruction. When bombs dropped from World War II airplanes hit the ground, piezoelectric crystals within the bombs' noses converted the mechanical pressure to the electrical charge needed to detonate the device.

JEWELLERY

The intrinsic beauty of gemstones and precious metals has led to their decorative use in all civilizations spanning thousands of years. In most societies jewellery was a sign of social rank. India and its surrounding countries were the main source of the great majority of gemstones within the ancient world. The tomb of Queen Pu-abi at Ur, dating back to 3000 BC, was believed to have contained the oldest examples of jewellery made of gold, silver, and the semi-precious carnelian, agate, and lapis lazuli.

Ancient caches of jewellery help to pinpoint when new mineral resources were discovered and highlight the prevailing fashion for particular gemstones. Citrine, for example, was rarely used before the Hellenistic era. Today, commercial concerns play a major part in dictating gem fashions. Cartier boosted citrine's popularity in the 1930s by producing a range of jewellery featuring it.

Egyptian makeup
Early Egyptians were the first civilization to develop the use of cosmetics. They indulged their love of greens and blues by highlighting their eyes with powdered malachite and lapis lazuli.

Quartz
The origin of the word "quartz" is uncertain, but it is thought to be a contraction of the German word "querklufterz", used to describe the transparent veins found in metal-mining areas.

◆

TALISMANS AND AMULETS

Amulets are worn because they are believed to have special properties. Among early civilizations they were thought to bring the wearer good luck, protect against misfortune, and ensure a departed soul's safe travel into the next life. Talismans are amulets that are engraved with astrological or occult symbols to enhance the power of the amuletic material. Any unusually shaped stone suggesting a link with a living object was considered amuletic. However, the symbolic power of gemstones, with their associations of royalty, influence, and wealth, enhanced amuletic potency. The colour of the mineral used was significant. Red stones, such as rubies, suggestive of blood, were believed to protect against wounding.

The animistic world view recognizes a living essence in everything. Early humans believed the world to be full of spirits who inhabited the natural environment. Only by appeasing these spirits with ritualistic precautions could a human hope to survive their mischief or take advantage of their good nature. However, the spiritual connection between humans and inanimate objects is not confined to pagan beliefs. In the Bible stones and rocks were a symbol of the human spirit and a representation of the higher Self. Christ is referred to as a "living stone".

An increasingly diverse number of attributes came to be bestowed on particular crystals over the centuries. Sapphires were not only a symbol of heavenly bliss (the blue variety being sky-coloured) but were also thought to protect against poverty, kill venomous creatures, prevent eye disorders, demonstrate faithfulness, and keep the wearer out of prison.

By the time that scientific materialism had taken hold in the second half of the 18th century, jewellery had lost most of its amuletic associations and was prized purely for its decorative and financial value. However, the belief that certain gemstones confer protection and good fortune still lies behind the contemporary custom of wearing birthstones (see pp.18-19).

Crystal spirits
Native Americans believed quartz crystals to be the home of supernatural forces that would bring good luck to their hunting expeditions. The Indians "fed" these spirits periodically by wiping the crystals with fresh deer's blood.

Protection
The custom of wearing protective amulets (below) and attributing special properties to commonplace objects was not without its sceptics. When the jester at the court of Holy Roman Emperor Charles V (1500-58) was asked what was the amuletic property of turquoise, he replied that if you happened to fall from a high tower while wearing it, the turquoise would remain unbroken.

CRYSTAL ENVIRONMENTS

Humans and the environment are mutually dependent. We rely on the earth for physical support, biological sustenance, and for spiritual inspiration. No civilization could have survived or developed without mineral resources.

Because the planet Earth represented life itself, primitive peoples endowed everything – animate and inanimate – with a soul or "living essence" in addition to its material form. Animism is the belief that all things, including the plant and mineral kingdoms, have a level of consciousness and is man's most ancient philosophy. From this belief has sprung countless rituals, myths, and legends about the spirits, good and bad, thought to inhabit all natural matter. Control of these spirits rested with the shaman, a tribal healer who mediated between the spirit world and humans.

SHAMANISM
Shamanism not only personalizes nature but views the human and natural worlds as reflections of each other. Shamans consider some areas on earth to be sacred places. These sacred spots exude more energy or "life force" than other localities.

Shamanism originated in Siberia and became the principal religion of early civilizations, spanning Russia, the Slavic countries, and parts of Scandinavia. It subsequently spread, and is still practised among cultures as diverse as the Native Americans, the Iban of Borneo, and the Aranta of central Australia. Aboriginal shamans are said to be initiated by ripping open their bodies and replacing the organs with crystals. The custom of cleansing crystals by "smudging" (see p.53) comes from the Native American practice of "empowering" natural objects by exposing them to the smoke of the sacred fire or tobacco.

Crystals are a key feature of the shaman's healing repertoire. They are thought to be the crystallized tears or semen of sky spirits. Shamans in northern Peru prepare a

Stones of the zodiac
Gemstones (right) have been assigned to each of the twelve months of the year and signs of the zodiac of the year since the Middle Ages. The practice of wearing gemstones is believed to relate back to the twelve stones on the breastplate of Aaron, brother of Moses, and is thought to bring good fortune .

There is no definitive list of birthstones (this list comes from Julia and Derek Parker's Astrology: read clockwise, starting at Aries, far right).

Aries – diamond
Taurus – emerald
Gemini – agate
Cancer –pearl
Leo – ruby
Virgo – sardonyx
Libra – sapphire
Scorpio – opal
Sagittarius – topaz
Capricorn – turquoise
Aquarius – aquamarine
Pisces – moonstone

healing table or "mesa" by dividing the area into three. One side of the table represents dark and evil magic. The opposite side symbolizes divine justice. The central area contains articles representing balance, in which a crystal is commonly placed. This middle zone is where the shaman exerts the greatest concentration to bring about the equilibrium necessary for healing.

CRYSTAL MYSTERY

The art of "scrying", or divining the future by using a crystal ball, pre-dates the Greek and Roman periods and has been common to many civilizations. The Ancient Japanese were particularly adept at fashioning perfect, polished spheres from rock crystal (clear quartz) or beryl. One of the largest ever produced was made from Madagascar rock crystal with a diameter of 15½ cm (6⅛ in). Transparent quartz continues to be the most popular material for crystal balls.

Crystal balls are said to produce visions when stared at for any length of time. The scientific explanation for this is that light reflected from a polished surface eventually exhausts the eye's sensitive optic nerve so that it stops transmitting an external image. This may account for the "disappearance" of the ball just before a vision and the fact that it is said to "mist over". Without an exterior impression to fix itself on, the eye then begins to respond to stimuli coming from the mind of the gazer. Persian writer, Ibn Kaldoun, expressed it more poetically when he wrote in 1332 about scrying: "The diviners while in this state do not see what is really to be seen. . . ; it is another kind of perception, which is born in them and which is realized not by sight but by the soul."

Crystals whose growth is interrupted sometimes produce a "phantom" effect, where parallel layers are housed inside the main growth. This can help to fuel the imagination of the scryer. Because of the rarity of perfectly transparent crystals, flawless balls are most likely to be plain glass rather than true crystal.

Feng Shui
In China the earth's subtle energy lines are known as "dragon paths". Feng Shui masters investigate the auspiciousness of a site before a house or office is built on it. Feng Shui, meaning "wind and water", conveys the Ancient Chinese principle of harmonizing humans and nature. This brings about good health, good fortune, and prosperity. To energize a home or room crystals should be placed in the south-west, north-west, or centre. Hanging clear crystals from a window infuses a room with re-vitalized, healthy "chi".

EARTH ENERGY

Without the noise and material distractions common to 20th-century living, early cultures "tuned in" more easily to earth's natural energy. The Swiss psychoanalyst, Carl Jung, believed that the unconscious mind was influenced by certain places and he called this "psychic localization".

The earth is a living organism. The Ancient Chinese recognized this and articulated an underlying energy they called "chi". There are three different kinds of chi. The first permeates our bodies (see p.99), another circulates the atmosphere, while the third flows through the earth itself. Earth chi is represented differently depending on the beliefs of the culture. In Europe it is synonymous with "ley lines", which were identified in 1921 by Englishman Alfred Watkins, who demonstrated that certain churches, ancient monuments, and some natural features such as hills could be "joined up" by an invisible straight line. This phenomenon is recognized worldwide. German archaeologists subsequently identified similar examples right across Europe and referred to them as channels of electromagnetic energy.

A matrix of "cosmic energy" was the subject of an investigation by three Russians – an historian, a construction engineer, and an electronics expert – in 1973. Their hypothesis was based on having traced a lattice-work pattern of electromagnetic energy that geometrically subdivided the earth's face into a combination of two shapes found naturally in crystals – an icosahedron and dodecahedron. These are two of the five Platonic Solids believed by the Ancient Greeks to hold the key to understanding the nature of the universe (see p.76). The positioning of these energy lines was claimed to explain various natural phenomena such as high and low barometric pressure areas, magnetic anomalies, and migration routes.

When envisioned as a crystal lattice over the earth's surface, this icosa-dodecahedron grid was also found to correspond with the birthplaces of ancient civilizations and monuments such as the Great Pyramid at Giza, the

The lodestone
The ingenuity with which humans have utilized certain unique characteristics of crystals is demonstrated by the invention of the compass. Magnetite – or the lodestone – is strongly magnetic. A piece floated on a stick in water was found by 12th-century mariners to align itself to the North Star.

◆

stone heads of Easter Island, and Machu Picchu in Peru. Some sources liken these "power centres" to the chakras of the human body, vortices of subtle energy, where channels of chi meet and cross (see pp.64-5).

GEOPATHIC STRESS

Naturally occurring radiation from within the earth, when distorted by underground water, certain mineral concentrations, and the foundations of human-made structures, is believed by medical practitioners around the world to cause "geopathic stress".

This natural phenomenon may result in a wide range of physical and mental conditions ranging from depression and insomnia to cancer and rheumatism. In the same way that overhead power cables may lower the immune system and promote illness in some areas, certain mineral concentrations coming into contact with underground streams may be capable of producing a build-up of harmful electromagnetic currents. Professional dowsers are occasionally called upon to detect where these adverse channels of electromagnetic energy are thought to be at their strongest.

Following sixty years of research in Germany into geopathic stress, some doctors take the effects so seriously that they test the homes of their most chronic patients for geopathic stress before going ahead with other treatments. Prevention and cure may be as simple a matter as moving the person's bed out of a harmful position.

RESONANCE

Crystals are forms which resonate and are capable of resonating in harmony with another form. In order for a sympathetic vibration to take place there must be a matching frequency and an overlap of energy between the two materials. Consider what happens when a tuning fork tuned to note A is sounded near a piano or guitar. Any string that is tuned to that same tone will pick up the vibration and resonate while the rest will not.

Stones of resonance
Stonehenge, in England, features eighty "blue stones" of dolorite which came originally from an area of Wales 200 km (124 miles) away.

Prehistoric humans appreciated the resonant qualities of crystalline materials. He constructed megaliths, or tribal burial chambers, according to the texture, weight, colour, and resonance of the stone. Using ropes, logs, and humanpower he transported huge stones by land and sea for vast distances.

One example of the resonant quality of Neolithic burial chambers was uncovered by a team of scientists representing Princeton University in the United States. Experimenting at the Newgrange megalith in Ireland (dating from 3500 BC), the team's instruments broadcast sounds at different frequencies until the lowest natural resonance of the internal chamber produced a detectable vibration. This resonant frequency was noted to have the same frequency as that produced by adult male voices. In the same way that you can get a "buzz" from singing or chanting in a large group, ancient man may have achieved the same by amplifying the sound of his voice within the resonating rocks.

Rock drawings inside and outside Newgrange were found to resemble the sine wave patterns derived from measuring different levels of resonance at the site. This is strongly suggestive that its builders knew a great deal more about the acoustical properties of various minerals than we may have thought possible, given the lack of instrumentation to record such phenomena. This may explain why Neolithic tribesmen travelled great distances and overcame enormous difficulties of transportation in order to find the exact material to meet their ritual needs.

Crystals in medical tradition
The concept of crystal healing played a major part in medical traditions from the Ancient Egyptians to the Renaissance (see chart below).

HISTORICAL ASSOCIATIONS

Hematite – an astringent suitable for eye problems.

Samian earth (kaolinite) – counteracts stomach ailments.

Pumice powder – used to treat sores when added to a poultice, also used as a toothpowder.

Garnet – red garnets were thought to be good for anaemia because they contain iron oxide.

Turquoise – a change of colour indicates the owner's state of health.

Diamond – bound to the left arm it cures nightmares.

Emerald – helps calm sore eyes when gazed at.

CRYSTAL TECHNOLOGY

Crystalline material is vital to a wide range of commercial and medical procedures, from construction to opticals, surgery to electronics. Diamonds that are not of gem quality are crushed up and used as scalpel tips and in dental drills. Most technological applications, though, require "perfect" synthetic crystals. Natural crystals contain naturally occurring flaws (known as "inclusions" – highly desirable for crystal healing, see p.80). In order to eliminate such imperfections for industrial use, man synthesizes crystals in a laboratory. Such crystals have the same atomic structure and properties as natural material, but are "engineered" to meet very specific criteria.

Silicon chips are used to receive, store, amplify, and transmit information in computers, credit and smart cards (see right), and the programmers of domestic appliances. While silicon is one of the most abundant materials on earth, it is unsuitable in its natural state for such delicate electronic devices because of the presence of impurities. Silicon has the important property of acting as both an insulator and as a conductor. It is therefore an ideal "semi-conductor". Pure, artificial silicon is "doped" with phosphorus, boron, or germanium to produce the different electrical charges required across different sections of a microchip.

Synthesized crystals used for industrial and medical purposes are produced using various methods, one of which was devised at the beginning of the 20th century. "Flame fusion" involves dropping powdered ingredients (in the case of ruby, aluminium, and chromium) into a furnace. The powder melts when it comes into contact with an oxygen flame of an extremely high temperature and fuses into drops of liquid. These drip slowly on to a rotating platform, where they go through the crystallization process, eventually producing a long, cylindrical crystal known as a "boule". Crystals produced using this method are of an extremely high quality and may also be cut as gems.

Smart cards
These have revolutionized the way we carry out day-to-day transactions, such as shopping and banking. Each card contains a minute, wafer-thin silicon chip which can store all sorts of information about the holder – from credit limits, financial transactions, and even health details.

◆

THE HEALING POWER OF CRYSTALS

The first known reference to the healing power of certain crystals comes from an Egyptian papyrus dated around 1600 BC, which gives directions for their curative use. Beads of lapis lazuli, malachite, and red jasper were worn around a sick person's neck so that the disease could pass through them and dissipate. The practice of placing or wearing stones on various areas of the body, with its amuletic links, was only part of the repertoire of healers in history. A particularly popular medicinal method was to pulverize gems, mix them with a liquid, and drink the result – the forerunner, perhaps, of mineral water.

The earliest-known writer on precious stones was the Greek philosopher Theophrastus (372-286 BC), author of *On Stones,* who extrapolated that stones could be distinguished sexually according to depth of colour.

Centuries later, in 1746, Sir John Hill, the English translator of Theophrastus' work, postulated that it was the metallic content of minerals which accounted for their curative powers. "Rogue" atoms of metals in some crystalline compositions are indeed responsible for the variety of colours available. Whether early civilizations knew of this link it is impossible to say, but certainly the mystical properties of gemstones were largely associated with colour. When hematite (from the Greek, *haima,* meaning blood) is crushed it produces a red powder. Hematite's healing properties were linked with blood-related conditions.

Many of Theophrastus' notions were repeated wholesale by Pliny the Elder (AD 23-79). The Greek was named by Pliny in his encyclopaedic work *Naturalis Historia.* Pliny was the investigative journalist of his day and his reportage gradually spanned the known world, to influence medical practice for the next 1500 years.

The universal belief in the benefits of gemstone medicine began to erode in the early 16th century. One of the catalysts may have been the first systematic attempt at viewing mineralogy as a science, put forward by Georgius Agricola (Georg Bauer, 1494-1555), a practising

Crystal skulls
Mysterious artefacts known as crystal skulls have been discovered across the world since the 1920s. In 1927 the first, known as the Mitchell-Hedges skull after the British explorer who found it, was unearthed in Belize. These skulls are generally full-sized reconstructions of human skulls made from quartz. Controversy surrounds them, particularly regarding their provenance. Some experts suggest that the skulls were fashioned by a highly advanced race, possibly "extra-terrestrial".

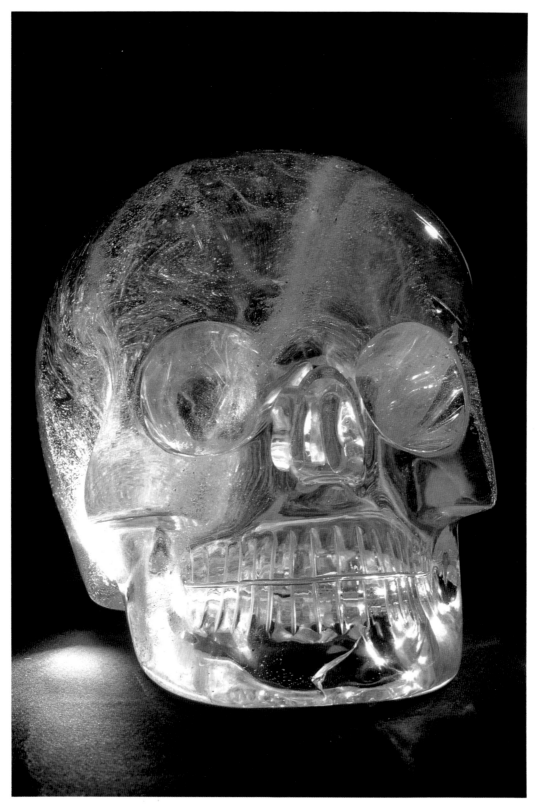

physician and metallurgist. His *De Re Metallica* was based purely on scientific research and observation. At the same time Swiss physician Paracelsus (1493-1541) was denouncing "quackery" and pointing to the adverse effects of minerals in drinking water by linking them with goitre. However, the practice of dispensing powdered gems persisted. According to the *Compleat Chymical Dispensary* of Dr John Schroder (1669) the best gems for healing were "granite", "hyacinth" (obsolete term for zircon or garnet), "sapphire, sardonyx and smaragde" (emerald). He reports that a few doctors of "real learning and repute" were offering scientifically based reasons for attributing curative powers to precious stones and metals.

Ineffectual remedies were blamed on bad apothecaries who substituted fake materials for profit. Cynicism in certain quarters persisted. One Veronese doctor, writing in the late 16th century, questioned the supposed medicinal properties of precious stones. He pointed out that, while they could be reduced to a powder, they could not be dissolved and therefore would not be absorbed by the body. However, his argument was confined only to the internal use of gems. He accepted that the stones had a subtle effect on the body when worn; close to the contemporary view that crystals can work with the body's subtle energy systems to bring about healing. The practice of taking gemstone powders internally continued in high society, as might be expected, considering the high cost of the raw ingredients.

By the beginning of the 20th century people were looking for a more scientific explanation for crystal healing. Dr William T. Fernie, writing *Precious Stones for Curative Wear and Other Remedial Uses* at the turn of the 20th century, quotes a "leading Medical Journal" which stated: "The astute physician should not altogether overlook the part taken by gems in the kaleidoscopic variation of human sentiments and the evolution of personal sympathies".

Shaping prisms
Pliny (see p.26) related that it was Indian gem cutters who were responsible for shaping the hexagonal prisms of beryls. Members of the beryl family, which include emerald, aquamarine, and heliodor, belong to the hexagonal crystal system (see p.38), whose common forms include hexagonal prisms. However it was nature that had fashioned these gemstones, not humans.

Fernie's book refers to a Professor Denton, who was said to be able to receive the stored memories of unspecified "geological specimens" by telepathic means. Fernie's personal view was that sunlight, electromagnetism, and also the composition of minerals rendered them beneficial to the open-minded. Several years later American gemmologist George Frederick Kunz linked his explanation of the therapeutic effects of precious stones taken internally to homeopathy. Kunz speculated that if smaller doses produced the greatest effect, then the "super subtle emanations" which came from precious stones would have even more powerful effects.

By the 1980s, Marcel Vogel, a respected authority on crystals, had placed the power of crystals firmly in the scientific domain. He suggested that the key to understanding this ancient knowledge lay in the connection between the vibrations sent out by the human mind and the perfect inner structure of crystals. Vogel was prompted to develop his investigations into crystal healing by working with liquid crystals in the laboratory. He found that by projecting a particular thought into liquid crystal it took on the shape of that thought. By thinking of a tree, for example, the growing crystal would take the shape of a tree. Sceptics point out, however, that some crystals do indeed grow in a dendritic shape suggestive of the branches of a tree. This is a particular property of theirs and has nothing to do with the "supernatural".

Rigorous scientific studies carried out currently by the Princeton Engineering Anomalies Research (PEAR) division in the United States, however, appear to validate Vogel's belief that the human mind can interact with, and affect, various inanimate objects and devices. PEAR's experiments show that human operators, with definite intentions, can produce statistically repeatable, consciousness-related, anomalous effects on machines such as random number generators. Which bodes well for those of us who frequently try our luck on the lottery. Perhaps all we have to do is concentrate a little harder.

Gem ingestion
Pope Clement VII, in the late 16th century, is reputed to have ingested a gem concoction worth 40,000 ducats – equivalent to more than two million pounds (three million dollars) today.

2

CRYSTAL SCIENCE

◆

"Nature has never made two human beings,
two plants or two crystals exactly alike.
Consider the magnitude of that diversity."

BARBARA WALKER, THE BOOK OF SACRED STONES

Our earth is 85% crystal. Its crust is largely silicon and oxygen, combined with six other common elements – aluminium, iron, calcium, sodium, potassium, and magnesium. From this chemical "casserole" comes an awe-inspiring variety of crystal colours, shapes, sizes, and hardness.

Earth is also the ultimate recycler – changing limestone to marble, or shale to garnet schist. A cocktail of ingredients form crystals under specific conditions of temperature, pressure, space, and time; yet when the conditions change the crystals may also be altered.

The reason why diamonds are found at only a few locations worldwide is because the exact conditions required for their formation are relatively rare. The high value we place on such gemstones is then heightened by the fact that large, perfect crystals are relatively scarce because of the complex and ever-changing circumstances taking place in nature.

Despite the vast abundance of minerals lying buried on this planet, human beings still need to synthesize crystals in the laboratory in order to meet the precise criteria for their technological needs.

Regardless of the many dramatic advances in science we find that replicating what nature does naturally and so easily is no mean feat. Certain aspects of the process of crystal formation within the earth still remain a mystery and perhaps will continue to be so for ever.

HOW CRYSTALS FORM

The largest variety of crystals, particularly those we value most – diamonds, rubies, sapphires – derive from molten rock, or magma. Magma is produced when the intense heat in the earth's core melts rocks in the upper mantle, or crust. As this molten "soup" of atoms cools and solidifies, it forms symmetrical, three-dimensional crystals.

Magma, which cools rapidly, may have insufficient time to form crystals and instead turns into amorphous material such as obsidian, a natural glass. Where the chemical composition is particularly complicated cryptocrystalline (*crypto* meaning hidden) material may also be produced.

As magma cools, the first crystals to form are those that have the highest melting points and relatively simple chemical composition. Gradually, different minerals form until only the more complex atoms are left. As these increase in concentration and the magma continues to cool, more elaborate crystals are produced.

Magma that reaches the surface of the earth as lava cools very quickly and produces amorphous material or rocks comprising tiny crystals. These are extrusive, or volcanic, igneous rocks – basalt is the most common kind. Magma held underground solidifies more slowly into coarse-grained rocks with larger, visible crystals. These are intrusive, or plutonic, igneous rocks – granite, the most common example, is composed mainly of quartz, feldspar, and mica.

Bubbles and films
Crystals that form very slowly rarely do so in a single, steady process. Tiny bubbles of gas or liquid, or a fine film of solid material, may enter the crystal during the successive stages of its development. These "inclusions" may contribute to the beauty and distinctiveness of the crystals they inhabit.

MOHS' SCALE
This scale of hardness is comparative – the intervals between one mineral and the next are not equal. Each mineral will scratch those below it and is scratched by those above.
1. Talc – scratched by fingernail
2. Gypsum – scratched by fingernail
3. Calcite – scratched by copper coin
4. Fluorite – scratched easily by pocket knife
5. Apatite – pocket knife just scratches it
6. Feldspar – scratched by steel file
7. Quartz – scratches window glass
8. Topaz – scratches quartz easily
9. Corundum – scratches topaz easily
10. Diamond – hardest natural material known

CRYSTALS FROM DISSOLVED MINERALS

Some of the finest examples of crystals, such as quartz and rhodochrosite, are formed from chemicals that have been dissolved in solutions within rock cavities. Here, they have both space and time to grow.

Water dissolves some minerals into their component ions (charged atoms) to produce an aqueous solution. Given the right conditions of time, temperature, and ingredients, the solution becomes over-saturated and precipitation of crystals takes place. The slower the precipitation, the bigger and better-formed the resulting crystals will be. Stalagmites and stalactites are examples of this form of crystallization.

Crystals produced from an aqueous solution either grow out from the centre or from the surface inwards. Agate, a variety of quartz, can form when silica-rich waters seep into cavities created by gas bubbles that become trapped in cooling magma. The silica is deposited in layers from the outside which gradually grow toward the centre. Agate that is not completely filled often has quartz crystals growing in this hollow space.

METAMORPHISM

Crystals are only stable within a specific range of conditions. Given the right chemical and physical conditions, they are susceptible to alteration. Change in pressure, temperature, or chemical conditions may cause a new species of mineral to form, one that is more stable within the changed environment. For example, blue turquoise may form when aluminium and phosphorus-rich minerals contact acidic, copper-bearing water.

Some minerals recrystallize in their solid state when extreme subterranean changes in temperature and pressure rearrange their atoms without any resultant melting. One example is the metamorphosis of limestone into marble and shales, which are altered to garnet-studded mica schist. The more varied the minerals in the original rocks, the greater the diversity of crystals that may result.

The quartz family
The name "quartz" does not just refer to a single crystal. It is also the generic term given to a large family of crystals. Each member belongs to the same crystal system (trigonal), shares the same chemical composition (silicon dioxide) and hardness (Mohs' scale 7 – see facing page), but otherwise exhibits individual properties. The quartz family comprises: rock crystal (clear quartz), amethyst, citrine, rose quartz, "smoky" quartz, aventurine quartz, milky quartz, tiger's eye, cat's eye, and hawk's eye.

CRYSTAL BIRTHPLACES

Some crystals, particularly the quartz varieties, are formed in many locations across the globe. Others, such as emerald and diamond, are formed in only a few. This map shows twenty of the most prized crystals and gemstones. Only a tiny proportion of crystals are considered to be of gem quality. The map highlights some of the major crystal deposits as well as where they are extracted in sufficient quantity and quality to make this work economically viable.

Canada
GOLD

California
GOLD

Ohio
CELESTITE

Southwestern USA
TURQUOISE

Colorado
LAPIS LAZULI

Arkansas
ROCK CRYSTAL

Sweden
HEMATITE

UK
CELESTITE

Poland
TURQUOISE

Germany
ROSE QUARTZ
CELESTITE
NEPHRITE

Italy
HEMATITE

Colombia
EMERALD

Chile
LAPIS LAZULI

Uruguay
AMETHYST
CARNELIAN

Brazil
ROCK CRYSTAL
TOURMALINE
AGATE
AQUAMARINE
ROSE QUARTZ
CARNELIAN
EMERALD
AMETHYST
CITRINE

Zaire
MALACHITE

West, Central & Southern Africa
DIAMOND

South Africa
GOLD
DIAMOND
TIGER'S EYE
EMERALD

Siberia
DIAMOND

Urals
CITRINE

Russia
HEMATITE
NEPHRITE
MALACHITE

China
AGATE

New Zealand
NEPHRITE

Afghanistan
LAPIS LAZULI

Kashmir
SAPPHIRE

Myanmar
TIGER'S EYE
RUBY

Pakistan
AQUAMARINE

Thailand
RUBY
SAPPHIRE

India
AGATE
CARNELIAN
AMETHYST

Iran
TURQUOISE

Sri Lanka
TOURMALINE
RUBY

Australia
AQUAMARINE
MALACHITE
TIGER'S EYE
DIAMOND
SAPPHIRE

SECONDARY DEPOSITS
The places where gemstones and other minerals are found are not
necessarily where they originally formed. As rocks are eroded or
broken away by wind and water, crystals become exposed at the
surface. They may then get washed out and transported down to
rivers or streams, where they form secondary, or "alluvial",
deposits which become trapped in pockets in the bends of streams.
Examples include rubies, spinels, and cat's
eye from Sri Lanka, and gold in the Yukon, Canada.

Madagascar
ROCK CRYSTAL
TOURMALINE
ROSE QUARTZ
CITRINE

NB: There are a great many more crystals and locations than can be
shown on this map. These twenty examples include many popular
healing crystals, some prized gemstones, and the precious metal,
gold. Only some of their major sources are indicated.

CRYSTAL STRUCTURE

The word "crystal" comes from the Greek "krystallos", meaning "ice". The Ancient Greeks gave this name to quartz because they believed that it was ice frozen so hard that it would never melt again. This legend was only exploded in the 18th century. Yet early writers were often nearer to certain truths about crystals than one might expect, given their lack of instrumentation. Pliny, in *Naturalis Historia*, writes of quartz: "It is not easy to find out why nature should build with six-angled bricks".

In 1784 René Just Haüy, a professor of mineralogy and crystallography in Paris, suggested that crystals were the result of minute, identical units. These "integral molecules" were, he postulated, stacked together in a regular manner, accounting for the smooth faces of crystals.

Crystalline materials as diverse as metal, sugar, kettle fur, and tooth enamel have one thing in common: an ordered internal structure of regularly repeating three-dimensional patterns. Even the most irregular or misshapen crystal shares this atomical neatness.

While smooth plane faces and geometric appearance are assumed to be the norm, such specimens only occur under extremely rare and ideal natural conditions. A crystal's external shape, or "habit", depends on its specific chemical ingredients, the conditions prevailing at the time of growth and the way the atoms are linked together. Different permutations of these result in crystals which form cubes, needles, fibres, plates, or masses.

Some minerals have exactly the same chemical composition but display very different forms and properties – they crystallize in different structures. Diamond and graphite are both made of elemental carbon. Diamonds comprise strongly bonded carbon atoms that form a rigid, compact structure, while the carbon in graphite lies in weakly bonded and widely spaced sheet-like layers.

The composition of some minerals varies from specimen to specimen. Tourmaline, for example, has a highly complex chemical composition in which components of similar size and valency can replace one another. While

Cleavage
In many varieties of crystal atoms are less strongly bonded in some planes, or parallel blocks of atoms, than others. Cleavage is a mineral's tendency to split when force is applied along this weakness (see below), leaving a flat surface. Crystals which do not cleave, such as quartz, may produce uneven surfaces, or "fractures", as a result of strong impact. Lapidaries use this knowledge when assessing how best to cleave a diamond, before cutting and polishing.

the structure or form of the crystal is not noticeably altered there can be wide variations in colour and hardness. Theoretically, 230 different three-dimensional crystal lattices could be represented in nature. In reality, there are only fourteen different, regularly ordered patterns in which crystals form. These are known as space lattices and are commonly depicted diagramatically as "balls and spokes" – the balls representing the atoms and the spokes the ionic bonds which hold them together.

SELF-REPLICATION

As a crystal forms, its external layer provides an atomic template for the next stage of growth. Only certain atoms, according to this optimum ordered structure, will bond with it. In the same way that a wall needs to have exactly the same basic shape and material of brick in order to produce a strong, solid structure, crystals will only add further layers that adequately match the original matrix, given the conditions of growth available.

CRYSTAL SYMMETRY

Crystal lattices are divided into seven basic crystal systems (see pp.38-9). These are further subdivided into 32 crystal classes – the number of different combinations of centres, planes, and axes of symmetry possible.

To determine the class of a crystal, you have to imagine a line passing through the centre of it. A centre of symmetry is present if every face, angle, or edge of a crystal has a diametrically opposite and similar one. A plane of symmetry divides an object in half so that the two halves are mirror images of each other.

An axis of symmetry denotes how many times the crystal appears to be the same when it is rotated 360 degrees. A two-fold axis of symmetry is repeated every 180 degrees, for example, and a three-fold repeats every 120 degrees.

Twinning
This is a common phenomenon of natural crystals, particularly quartz. Changes of temperature or pressure affecting a mineral can cause its crystal lattice to "flip over". It may then grow in two different directions from one original face, producing a right-angled "twin".

◆

THE SEVEN CRYSTAL SYSTEMS

Crystal shapes – or forms – are determined by their internal atomic order and classified according to shape and symmetry into one of the following seven crystal systems.

◆ CUBIC/ISOMETRIC: e.g. DIAMOND, GARNET
Common forms include: cube, octahedron. This system has the highest degree of crystalline symmetry, with three axes of equal length that meet at right angles.
9 planes of symmetry, 13 axes, and a centre of symmetry

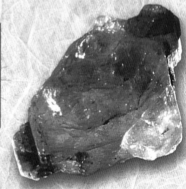

◆ HEXAGONAL: e.g. EMERALD, AQUAMARINE
Common forms include: prism, bipyramid. This system has four axes, a vertical or "principal" axis, which is longer or shorter than the other three, which are equal and intersect at 60 degrees.
7 planes of symmetry, 7 axes, and a centre of symmetry

◆ TETRAGONAL: e.g. ZIRCON, RUTILE
Common forms include: four-sided prism, tetragonal bipyramid.
This system has three axes all at right angles to each other, two of which are equal in length and the third which is either longer or shorter than them.
5 planes of symmetry, 5 axes, and a centre of symmetry

◆ TRIGONAL: e.g. QUARTZ, SAPPHIRE
Common forms include: prism,
rhombohedron.
This system is sometimes included in the
hexagonal system as it can be referred to
by the four crystal axes of that system.
*3 planes of symmetry, 4 axes, and a centre
of symmetry*

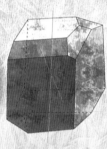

◆ TRICLINIC: e.g. TURQUOISE,
SUNSTONE
Only common form is pinacoid (pair of
faces parallel to two axes).
This system has three axes of unequal
length intersecting each other obliquely.
*No planes of symmetry or axes, but a
centre of symmetry*

◆ ORTHORHOMBIC: e.g. PERIDOT, TOPAZ
Common forms include: rhombic prism,
pyramid and dome terminations.
This system has three axes all at 90-degree
angles to each other, of unequal length.
*3 planes of symmetry, 3 axes, and a centre
of symmetry*

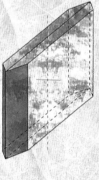

◆ MONOCLINIC: e.g. JADEITE,
MOONSTONE
Common forms include: prism, pinacoid.
This system has three axes of unequal
length, two of which intersect at oblique
angles to each other and the third, which is
perpendicular.
*1 plane of symmetry, 1 axis, and a centre of
symmetry*

CRYSTALS AND LIGHT

Theories about visible light and its connection with colour have been expressed since the days of Plato and Aristotle. However, the first known systematic examination of how crystals react to light was written in the late 17th century by Dutch scientist Christiaan Huygens in *Treatise on Light*.

When white light hits a transparent crystal or glass prism it is split into its seven constituent colours – the "rainbow" spectrum of red, orange, yellow, green, blue, indigo, and violet. Such dispersion of light with regard to gemstones is known as "fire", or brilliance. Diamonds and other precious gems are cut, or "faceted", to enhance this natural quality.

The passage of light through crystals determines whether we see them as coloured (where some light is absorbed) or colourless (where no light is absorbed).

REFLECTION AND REFRACTION

The behaviour of light meeting a crystal depends very much on that mineral's particular chemical composition and structure. It presents gemmologists with a means of distinguishing one specimen from another. We describe the appearance of the surface of a crystal, which depends on the amount of light reflected, as its "lustre". Most crystals have a vitreous (i.e. glass-like) lustre.

As light passes from one medium (e.g. air) to another (e.g. a solid crystal) the light rays change direction; they are bent, or "refracted"(see the Refractive Index, above right). Crystals from the cubic system (e.g. diamond, garnet, fluorite) and all amorphous material allow light to pass through in all directions with the same refraction. They are said to be "singly refractive"(see the illustration, above right).

Other crystalline material is "doubly refractive" (see the illustration, lower right). Light entering these crystals travels along two pathways that vibrate at right angles to each other. All crystals from the six crystal systems other than cubic are doubly refractive. The effect is particularly

The Refractive Index (RI)
This is the degree to which light rays bend as they enter or leave a crystal. The more the light bends, the greater the RI. Gemmologists use RI to identify crystals. RI can help distinguish between a red spinel (singly refractive) and ruby (doubly refractive), which superficially resemble one another.

Single refraction

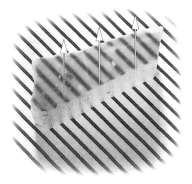

Double refraction

dramatic in calcite, or "Iceland spar". If a block of calcite is placed over a line of writing the words appear double.

CRYSTAL COLOURS

The colour of some crystals is due to light-absorbing atoms that are an intrinsic part of their chemical structure. Examples include malachite, which is always green, lapis lazuli and azurite, which are blue, and sulphur, which is yellow. The stability of the crystal structure means that it is almost impossible deliberately to interfere with their colour through heating or irradiation without destroying the crystal itself.

The majority of minerals, however, contain "rogue" atoms, minute impurities – usually metals – within their chemical structures. These trace elements contribute to the wide range of colours perceived. The beryl family, whose shared composition is beryllium aluminium silicate, include green emeralds (due to the presence of chromium), yellow heliodor (iron), and pale rose to violet morganite (manganese). As a general rule the greater the amount of trace impurities contained within the crystal, the deeper the colour appears.

Many gemstones can be heat-treated or irradiated to enhance their colour. Aquamarine is one example. While historically it was valued for its natural sea-green hue, today aquamarine is most valued when sky or dark blue. Careful heating produces this colour effect, while overheating will render it colourless.

One can see a variety of colour effects within a single crystal, depending on the angle at which it is viewed. Tourmaline, aquamarine, and morganite, for example, look a different colour, or shade of colour, when viewed from different directions. When aquamarine is held up and viewed at one angle it will appear colourless, at another it will look blue.

Agate banding
All agates have distinctive colour bands. These are due to chance variations in the distribution of pigmented impurities as the mineral progressively solidified. The most common trace elements within agates are iron compounds. These give some agates their distinctive red-brown colour. Every agate is unique and even specimens growing in close proximity to one another reveal quite different colouring and patterned bands.

CRYSTAL ELECTRICITY

Certain crystals, most notably the quartz family, can convert mechanical pressure into electrical energy – the stylus on a record player is a good example of this. They can also convert electrical energy into precise mechanical vibrations, as in earphones and ultrasonic radiators. This is known as the piezoelectric effect, from the Greek word, *piezo*, meaning "to press", and was discovered by French scientists Pierre and Jacques Curie, in 1880.

When mechanical pressure is applied to quartz crystals (silicon dioxide), the crystal lattice becomes temporarily deformed. The positive silicon ions move to one side of the crystal, while the negative oxygen ions move to the other side. This results in the opposite faces developing different and powerful electrical charges. However, this is not the same as generating an electric current. Non-metallic minerals do not conduct electricity. The relatively rigid structures of most of them allow their component atoms very little room for manoeuvre. As a result, they do not have the loose electrons needed to conduct an electric current.

While natural quartz is abundant it is rarely perfect, rendering it unsuitable for industrial use. Piezoelectric crystals are therefore produced synthetically in the laboratory. They have exactly the same atomic structure and properties as their natural counterparts but are designed to meet very precise criteria. Piezoelectricity is a valuable property commercially and has been extensively used since first discovered. During World War I the piezoelectric effect was used to produce underwater acoustic waves as an early form of submarine-detector sonar.

QUARTZ TIMEPIECES

The atoms within micro-thin slices of synthetic quartz for watches and clocks vibrate at 32,768 times per second. The crystal requires very little power, which is supplied by a tiny battery or an accumulator in the case of solar-powered devices. As the atoms in the quartz vibrate they emit very precise electronic pulses. These pulses are

Pyroelectricity

Crystals such as tourmaline and quartz develop electric charges on their opposing faces when they are heated. This effect is known as pyro-electricity. A pyroelectric thermometer is an instrument which is used to determine the temperature change in certain crystalline material by measuring the voltage produced when its electrical charges separate.

How to demonstrate piezoelectricity

Take two quartz crystals (right) with no terminations and at least one flat, unpolished, side. Two nuggets of rose quartz are ideal. In a dark room, rub or bang the two flat sides of the crystals together. Friction causes the quartz to light up. Do not attempt this with prized crystals or those with flaws.

channelled through microchip circuitry, where they are successively halved in a series of fifteen steps. The result is a single, constant pulse per second.

An "inverse" piezoelectric effect is produced when a quartz plate is subjected to an alternating electrical charge. The crystal will start alternately to expand and contract, during which it vibrates at a precise frequency. Arranged for this purpose, a circuit called a crystal oscillator controls the frequency bands in radio transmitters.

NANOTECHNOLOGY

In the past scientists have been concerned with determining various aspects of crystal structure. In the future they will manipulate such structures atom by atom. Molecular manufacturing, or "nanotechnology", is being researched in various parts of the world.

Nanotechnology involves the precise placement of individual atoms in order to produce a calibre of manufacturing that was once unimaginable. While all manufactured products are made from atoms, current "bulk" technology involves assembling such products part by part. Nanotechnology has been described as taking off the boxing gloves so that nature's atoms can be inexpensively assembled into any desired arrangement.

This technological revolution goes back less than 40 years, inspired by American physicist Richard Feynman in 1959, who envisioned the possibility of rearranging objects atom by atom. However, nanotechnology is not just about making smaller products but about extending the precise control of molecular structure to big things.

Work is under way to produce the computer-aided design (CAD) tools necessary for the manipulation of crystalline material, particularly diamond. Diamond is the hardest natural substance known to man, yet it is light in relation to metals such as steel. Nanotechnology has far-reaching implications for many commercial enterprises, including the airline industry. One intention is to build, from diamond-like material, aircraft that are

Quartz for keeping time
Quartz has revolutionized the watch and clock industry, making such timepieces accessible to almost everyone. Their timekeeping performance is excellent and, without the need for a complicated internal assembly, they can be produced very cheaply. The performance of quartz clocks has only been surpassed with the advent of atomic clocks.

one-hundredth the weight but ten thousand times the
strength they are at present.

Diamond and graphite – the one hard, the other soft –
are two forms of pure elemental carbon. It is the precise
structure of its atoms that accounts for diamond's extra-
ordinary properties. In Japan, a nanotechnological race is
on to make diamond from natural gas at low pressure.

In the late 1980s, scientists discovered new molecules
that represented a third form of carbon. As a group, these
molecules are called fullerenes. One member of the
group, buckminsterfullerene, has a perfectly spherical
molecule composed of 60 carbon atoms. Known
colloquially as "bucky balls", these molecules are thought
to be abundant in interstellar dust, in the soot from fires,
and in the freshly lit flame of a candle.

One of the goals of nanotechnology is to enable manufacturing costs to be cheaper, involving only the price of
raw materials and the energy needed to manipulate their
atomic structure. CAD tools allow an operator to edit out
individual atoms or groups of atoms using computer-
generated "selection lattices" in order to change or add to
the overall bonding structure. Predictions suggest that
within twenty years full manufacturing capability using
nanotechnology will be a reality. The start of the next
millennium may well be referred to as the Diamond Age.

ORGANIC CRYSTALS

The advent of nanotechnology moves humanity a step
closer to what nature achieves on a daily basis. One theory to emerge from new science is that the self-replicating
properties of crystals (see p.37) may have been
instrumental in the development of organic molecules,
such as amino acids and DNA, and hence life on Earth.
The fact that living things possess biomagnetic fields, or
auras, lends credence to the suggestions that the self-
replicating crystals responded to vibrations from a super-
energy field permeating the cosmos.

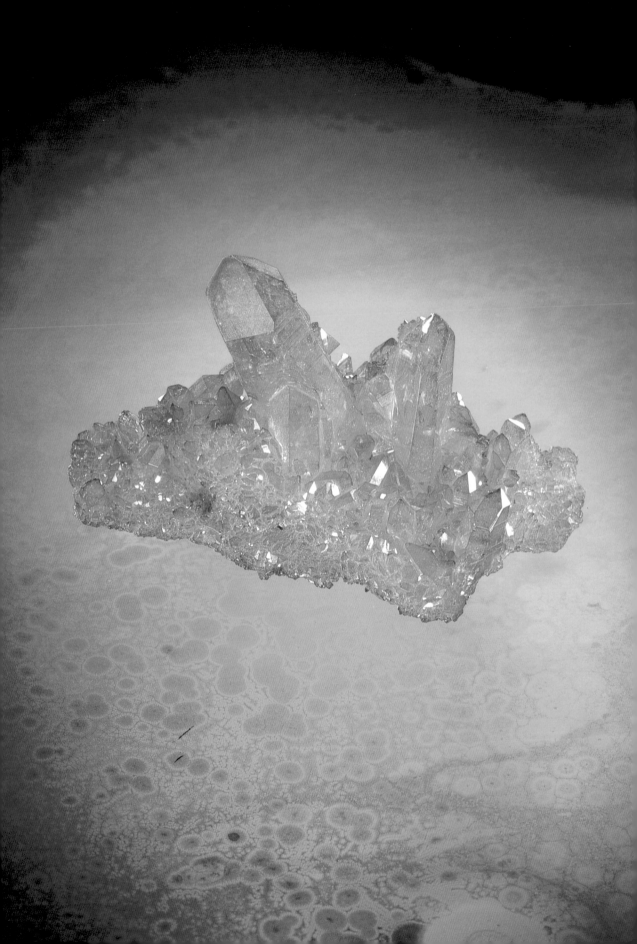

3

CRYSTAL INSIGHT

◆

"A life of wisdom must be a life of contemplation combined with action."

M. SCOTT PECK, THE ROAD LESS TRAVELLED

Chapters One and Two explored the historical and scientific relevance of crystals, but we now take a leap into territory which science is currently at a loss to explain – how crystals can play a part in healing. Because of their inherent neatness, crystals are a metaphor for perfect order and balance. They represent the equilibrium we seek to achieve in our lives and which results in good health. The combination of perfect form and energy are the processes through which crystals encourage our bodies to come into balance and why they are such powerful tools for self-healing.

However, the principles which underpin the use of crystals for healing purposes are quite different from those utilized by technology. While industry synthesizes crystals for its particular needs, crystal healers use stones formed by nature in order to enjoy a tangible connection with the Earth and to tap in to the energies of the mineral kingdom. Whereas technologically crystalline material receives and transmits a form of electrical energy, it is scientifically immeasurable "subtle energies" which crystals channel and amplify through the body in order to bring about healing in many forms.

The chances are that you already have one or more crystals in your possession. The advice in this chapter aims to help you to add to your crystal collection by prompting you to think carefully about the different ways in which crystals can play a part in your own healing process.

SOME QUESTIONS ABOUT CRYSTALS

Many crystal healers believe that choosing a crystal is largely intuitive. The crystal you acquire is the one you are "meant" to have. However, you can save yourself time and expense by thinking about why you want a crystal and what kind you prefer. These "open questions" are designed to help you focus on your choice. There are no rights or wrongs about working with crystals; it is your personal relationship with them that is the vital thing.

◆ What do you want the crystal for – physical healing, meditation, energizing your home or workplace, as a focus for visualization, or for decorative inspiration?

◆ Which crystals are the most appealing to you – geometrically shaped, such as clear quartz, or "massive", such as rose quartz?

◆ Which colours are you attracted to? Are you drawn to pale or deep shades?

◆ What size of crystal are you looking for? Small ones are suitable for body layouts; larger ones are good for meditation.

◆ Do you prefer clear or opaque crystals?

◆ Have you thought about including a specially configured quartz crystal in your collection (see pp.50-1)?

◆ Do you prefer cut and polished crystals or ones that are completely natural?

◆ Are you drawn to crystals with particular optical qualities, e.g. "rainbows"?

◆ Do you think of inclusions as being "flaws" or enhancements ?

◆ How much are you prepared to spend?

◆ Would you prefer lots of cheaper tumble-stones or a few, more expensive, crystals?

◆ How do you feel about crystals that have been heat-treated to enhance their colour (e.g. aqua aura, citrine, aquamarine)?

◆ Would you prefer to own crystals that you can wear (e.g. as a pendant)?

◆ If your crystals are to be handled regularly, have you thought about their texture?

◆ Will your crystals be private or are you happy to display them? Where will you put them? How they will look?

◆ How do you feel about waiting until you find a crystal you really connect with?

◆ Are you happy to accept a crystal as a gift, or do you prefer to choose your own?

◆ Do you have a particular crystal supplier in mind? Are you sure that this source is reputable and sells genuine crystals? Get a recommendation from a crystal healer or workshop teacher if you can.

GOOD VIBRATIONS

The senses are vitally important when selecting crystals, whether for body layouts, meditation, or simply to "lift" the energies of your surroundings. Regardless of the selection, one crystal will catch your eye. Pick this one up, but then take time to "feel" whether it is right for you, both intuitively and physically. Crystal healing relies on the optimum relationship between mental and crystal energy. If you are unsure replace the crystal and look again. This is similar to being introduced to a new group of people. There are some individuals you are immediately drawn to; others you are unsure about or dislike on sight. The common factor between choosing friends and crystals can be summed up in two words – "good vibrations". Even if you leave the shop empty-handed, you have made the right choice. Better luck next time.

THE REAL THING?

Neither imitation nor synthetic crystals are suitable for healing. Crystal healing and meditation are based on tuning in to the natural vibrations of a mineral from the Earth which is imbued with its energies. Imitation crystals can be glass or plastic, which is not crystalline and plays no part in crystal healing. Sometimes natural minerals are sold as entirely different crystals, and crystals balls are often clever glass imitations. The give-away is that while most crystal contains natural inclusions, glass is too perfect. You can also tell by holding the object; natural quartz remains cold for longer.

Synthetic crystals have exactly the same composition, and near-identical optical and physical properties, as natural crystals. Synthetics are difficult to spot without advanced instrumentation because they so closely resemble natural crystals. Some crystals are treated to deepen the colour. There is no rule about using colour-enhanced, natural crystals; some crystals are found in limited colours only, while others demonstrate a range. Colour is important when working with chakras (see pp.68-9).

Tips for choosing crystals

◆ *When faced with a number of crystals, close your eyes and visualize your ideal one. Open your eyes and pick up the first one you are drawn to.*

◆ *Hold your hand over the crystals. If you feel a slight "magnetic pull" or tingling over one particular crystal, that is a sign to choose it; your energetic vibrations are compatible.*

◆ *If you have to rely on mail order, try to establish a good rapport with the person you speak to before placing your order.*

CRYSTAL CONFIGURATIONS

Members of the quartz family – such as rock crystal (clear quartz), amethyst, and rose quartz – are the most important crystals used in healing. Rock crystal is particularly versatile and can be used for any healing purpose on all the chakras. Quartz also occurs in many different configurations, which are believed by esoterists to generate specific energy frequencies. The following are some of the most common ones:

◆ SINGLE-TERMINATORS
These are six-sided quartz crystals whose faces join to form an apex at one end. The other end is usually rough, where it has broken away from its source. Large single-terminators with a wide base, allowing them to stand, are called "generators". These are believed to represent the perfect geometric form through which universal energy can flow. The direction of the terminated point indicates energy flow. Smaller single-terminators are used in layouts to concentrate and direct healing energy from one chakra to another.

◆ DOUBLE-TERMINATORS
These crystals have pointed terminations at both ends. Double-terminators represent the uniting of opposites – positive and negative, yin (female) and yang (male), life and death. They are recognized as simultaneous transmitters and receivers of energy and are used in healing layouts to unblock negative energy. In meditation they can symbolize the balance of spirit with matter.

◆ TABULAR CRYSTALS

"Tabbies" are flattened columnar crystals in which two of the six sides are wider. They may be single- or double-terminated or form part of a cluster. Tabular crystals are used extensively for telepathic healing and communication. They are used in healing layouts as a "bridge" between two points, such as balancing energies between two individuals or two chakras. Tabbies are believed to turn up at important stages in personal development, when help is needed to cross to the next level of awareness.

◆ RAINBOW CRYSTALS

"Rainbows" occur in both transparent and opaque crystals. They are caused by internal fractures which interfere with white light, splitting it into seven colours of the spectrum. Rainbows symbolize life containing sadness ("rain") and happiness ("sunshine"). In healing, rainbow crystals are valuable for disappointment or depression. Placed on the heart chakra the rainbow can help imbue joy.

◆ CLUSTERS

Clusters are two or more single-terminated quartz crystals sharing a common base, representing an evolved community of individual crystals on common ground, reaping the benefits of peace and harmony. These crystals are said to emit intensified healing and cleansing vibration. In a workplace they encourage and enhance co-operation.

CLEANSING AND TUNING

Cleanse new crystals straight away, particularly if you intend to use them for healing. Cleansing is not a physical process: rather a spiritual ritual. In esoteric terms crystals absorb and retransmit all energies with which they come into contact. In healing crystals become receptive to emotional energies. Cleansing brings your crystal back to a neutral state, so that accumulated negative energies are not passed on. This process also re-energizes the crystal and ensures that it functions at its highest level. Let your intuition be the best guide: keep the intention in mind that you are clearing away all inappropriate energies and that you are working with purity of purpose. (NB Some crystals are sensitive to light and water – see pp.54-5.)

◆ SUNLIGHT
Light is the essential currency of crystal healing, so re-energize your water-cleansed stones in sunlight for 24 hours before dedicating them.

◆ RUNNING WATER
Cleanse your crystals by holding them under running water, such as an ordinary bathroom tap. As you do so, think about a beautiful waterfall you have seen or visited. Or imagine the waves lapping over your crystal on a tropical beach.

◆ RESONATING SOUND
Purify your crystals with the resonating sound of a bell you love. You can cleanse a roomful of crystals by ringing the bell above them, but the best way is to purify crystals one at a time.

◆ SMUDGING
"Smudge" your crystals by burning a wadge of dried herbs and waving the smoke over and through them. You can use smudging to purify a roomful of crystals.

◆ EARTH BURIAL
Crystals have come from the earth. If you feel they are safe enough you can bury your crystals in the ground (mark where you have left them). The earth has a natural, magnetic quality which will draw off negativity.

◆ CRAB APPLE AND SEA SALT
Soak crystals in a non-metallic container filled with water to which some purifying sea salt or crab apple Bach Flower Remedy has been added. Clean sea water is another option. Some people suggest leaving the container on a window ledge for three days before the full moon.

◆ THOUGHT VISUALIZATION
Imagine a bright star pouring pure white light through an opening in the top of your head. Guide it down through your body, sensing it being cleansed. Feel negative energies draining out of your feet. Now dedicate the crystal: "I dedicate this crystal to love and for the universal benefit of all".

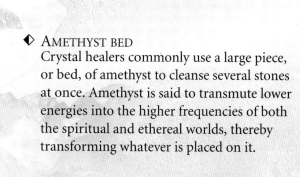

◆ AMETHYST BED
Crystal healers commonly use a large piece, or bed, of amethyst to cleanse several stones at once. Amethyst is said to transmute lower energies into the higher frequencies of both the spiritual and ethereal worlds, thereby transforming whatever is placed on it.

CLEANSING BY THOUGHT VISUALIZATION

Crystals are activated by the thought energy of their guardian, acting as catalysts in the healing process. But you are fundamental in bringing about your own healing, so it is vital to engage your mind and pay attention to thoughts in visualization, which you should adapt to your own needs.

Sit comfortably in a peaceful spot, both feet on the floor to "ground" yourself (see p.81). Lay the crystal on an outstretched palm or clench it with the terminated end upward. Close your eyes, take a few deep breaths and follow the thought visualization on page 53. This puts it on "standby" so that it can be "switched on" as soon as it is tuned (see below and facing page).

IS YOUR CRYSTAL SENSITIVE?

Many crystals are sensitive to light, heat, or water. Check the list (facing page) before deciding on a cleansing method (see pp.52-3). Some crystals are also relatively soft. If you use salt, ensure that it has dissolved completely before immersing your crystals, otherwise the grains may scratch softer material. See page 32 for the relevant Mohs' scale number, which is shown alongside the list of easily scratched crystals. The quartz family (Mohs 7) comprises hard, tough minerals which can withstand heat and immersion in water. However, those within the chalcedony groups, such as agate, may be dyed or stained. Check that the colour is water-resistant by applying a cotton ball dampened with water to the reverse side before leaving agate to soak in water. Never use chemicals, ultrasonic cleaners, or steamers.

TUNING YOUR CRYSTALS

Crystal healers use a variety of expressions to describe a crystal for a specific purpose such as healing or meditation. Some healers consider "tuning" to be the same as "dedicating". Others refer to the tuning process as "energizing" or "programming" their crystals.

Tuning your crystal is analogous to preparing to listen to a radio broadcast. When you cleanse and dedicate your crystals you are "switching them on". When you tune them, you are selecting the desired wavelength. Tuning a crystal involves having the intention to use the crystal for a particular purpose. This is a complementary process. You are assisting the crystal to serve its particular purpose, while the crystal helps you correct any physical, mental, or emotional imbalance.

It is a good idea to work with a crystal for one purpose only. For example, amethyst is an excellent crystal for meditation, as is rock crystal (clear quartz), with its inner "landscapes" or "inclusions". It is better to separate the crystals you will use for healing, meditation, or dream work and tune them accordingly. Otherwise it is like listening to one radio station broadcasting two different programmes simultaneously. You will not get the full benefit of either. Tuning each crystal individually makes it easier to remember its particular purpose.

How to tune
It is important to tune directly after cleansing and dedicating (see pp.52-3).
◈ *Remain in a relaxed, alert state.*
◈ *Hold your crystal in one hand and place the other over it.*
◈ *Visualize an energy connection between you and the crystal (e.g. a ray of white light).*
◈ *Decide on the crystal's purpose. Then say: "I intend this crystal to be an effective tool for. . . (e.g. healing, meditation, or interpreting dreams)".*

CRYSTAL SENSITIVITY
Avoid contact with water:
Halite – water soluble
Selenite – water soluble
Lapis lazuli – porous, do not soak, dry after cleansing
Malachite – cool water only
Turquoise – do not soak
Light-sensitive crystals
Amethyst – may fade
Rose quartz – may fade
Turquoise – may dry out and fade

Heat-sensitive crystals
Amethyst – may fade in gentle heat, become colourless in strong heat
Quartz – may fracture with sudden temperature changes
Lapis lazuli – avoid high heat
Malachite – avoid sudden temperature changes
Tourmaline – high heat alters colours
Turquoise – sensitive to all heat

Crystals that are easily scratched (Mohs' no. alongside – see p.32):
Metallic crystals (e.g. gold 2½-3)
Celestite (3-3½)
Malachite (3½-4)
Rhodochrosite (3½-4)
Fluorite (4)
Apatite (5)
Lapis lazuli (5-6)
Sodalite (5-6)
Turquoise (5-6)
Hematite (5½-6½)
Moonstone (6-6½)

◆

TWENTY KEY CRYSTALS

The following list (pp.56-7 and 60-1) suggests twenty different crystals with which to undertake a wide range of crystal work. Refer also to the numbered photographs on pp.58-9 and 62-3.

Key for numbered photographs: **1** = Lapis lazuli; **2** = Hematite; **3** = Citrine; **4** = Agate; **5** = Rose quartz; **6** = Malachite; **7** = Sodalite; **8** = Carnelian; **9** = Amethyst; **10** = Rock crystal (clear quartz); **11** = Bloodstone; **12** = Aventurine quartz; **13** = Watermelon tourmaline; **14** = Tiger's eye; **15** = Moonstone; **16** = Turquoise; **17** = Jade; **18** = Celestite; **19** = Aquamarine; **20** = Fluorite.

Each description covers (as far as possible):
◆ Derivation of name
◆ Crystal "family"
◆ Chemical composition
◆ Colours
◆ Special notes on buying or using
◆ Historical use
◆ Associated words or phrases linked to contemporary healing use
◆ Associated chakras (see also pp. 64-5 and 68-9).

AGATE (see no.4, p.58): Named after a river in southern Sicily.
Cryptocrystalline quartz (chalcedony); silicon dioxide; distinctive banded patterns and colours which vary according to different impurities. Many different forms, e.g. moss agate, fire agate, and blue-laced agate.
Special note: Often dyed to enhance colour.
Historical use: Thought to guarantee plentiful crops, cure insomnia, ward off skin diseases.

Associated words/phrases: Stabilizing; balancing; enhances self-esteem; calms body and mind; promotes inner peace; assists physical and emotional security.
Chakras: Base, Throat.

AMETHYST (see no. 9, p.59): from Greek, *amethystos,* meaning "unintoxicating".
Quartz family; silicon dioxide; pale lavender to deep violet.
Special note: Dichroic (two different shades according to angle viewed).
Historical use: In Ancient Greece and Rome wine was drunk from cups of carved amethyst because it was believed to cure drunkenness and bring general sobering.
Associated words/phrases: Calming; cleansing; transformational; promotes spiritual awareness and contentment; excellent for meditation; aids sleep; absorbs negativity; combats atmospheric pollution.
Chakras: Third eye, Crown.

AQUAMARINE (see no.19, p.63): from Latin, *aqua marina,* meaning "sea water".
Beryl family; beryllium aluminium silicate; various shades of blue or green.
Special note: Usually heat-treated to produce the more popular deep-blue colour; dichroic.
Historical use: Amulets worn for protection and good luck by sailors and fishermen. Recommended for head and neck problems.
Associated words/phrases: Mental clarity; self-expression; "stone of courage"; eases fears and phobias; calming; stress reducing; enhances creativity; protects against pollutants.
Chakra: Throat.

AVENTURINE QUARTZ (see no.12, p.62): from Italian, *per avventura,* meaning "by accident" (given same name as accidentally produced glass of similar appearance).
Quartz family; silicon dioxide; yellowy-brown to bluish-green, depending on inclusions.

Special note: Easy to confuse with aventurine feldspar (sunstone), amazonite, and jade. Look for inclusions, which give it a sparkly appearance.
Historical use: Said to encourage Lady Luck to call, particularly with regard to money.
Associated words/phrases: All-purpose healing stone; promotes physical, mental, and emotional well-being; enhances personal creativity and originality; stress-relieving; soothing.
Chakras: Sacral, Solar plexus, Heart.

BLOODSTONE (HELIOTROPE) (see no.11, p.62):

Cryptocrystalline quartz (chalcedony); silicon dioxide; always opaque, dark green spotted with red (iron oxides) resembling drops of blood, hence the name.
Historical use: Considered a stone to aid clairvoyance, especially foretelling of extremes of weather. Said to check hemorrhages.
Associated words/phrases: Detoxifying; purifying (particularly with regard to blood); strengthening; improves talents and abilities; enhances decision-making insight.
Chakra: Base.

CARNELIAN (see no.8, p.59): from Latin, *carne,* meaning "flesh".

Cryptocrystalline quartz (chalcedony); silicon dioxide; always translucent, reddish-brown.
Historical use: Recommended for blood disorders, to calm anger and inflammation in connection with its red colour.
Associated words/phrases: Focusing; motivational; stimulating; dispels apathy; increases physical energy and personal power; engenders compassion; encourages present-moment awareness.
Chakras: Sacral, Alter major (part of "New Age" expanded chakra system, located in nasal area).

CELESTITE (see no.18, p.63): from Latin, *caelestis,* meaning "heavenly".

Strontium sulphate; colourless, pale blue, milky white, orange, yellow.
Special note: Extremely soft and fragile.
Historical use: Used by Bengali priests to colour flames (produced by the element strontium) and impress or frighten followers.
Associated words/phrases: Revitalizing; awakens spirituality; elevating; regenerative; ensures fluency in communication; useful for dream recall.
Chakras: Throat, Crown.

CITRINE (see no.3, p.58): from Latin, *citrus,* – pale greenish-yellow colour.

Quartz family; silicon dioxide; yellow-brown.
Special note: Most "citrine" sold in shops is heat-treated amethyst – check suppliers.
Historical use: One of the "merchant's stones" believed to help accumulate and maintain wealth if kept in cash box or purse.
Associated words/phrases: "group" stone that positively influences family, business, friendships, etc.; encourages openness; optimistic; dispels fear; promotes physical endurance and mental clarity; cleansing; supports emotional maturity.
Chakras: Sacral, Solar plexus.

FLUORITE (see no.20, p.63): from Latin, *fluor,* meaning "to flow".

Calcium fluoride; wide range of colours, including – violet, green, yellow, blue, pink, and purple.
Special note: Soft, easily scratched; fluorescent.
Historical use: Believed to benefit teeth and bones when taken as an elixir. Also said to relieve symptoms of kidney disease.
Associated words/phrases: Protective; energizing; grounding; releases negativity and emotional "blockages"; calming; promotes mental advancement; good for meditation.
Chakra: Third eye.

TWENTY KEY CRYSTALS (NUMBERS 1 TO 10)

TWENTY KEY CRYSTALS (CONTINUED)

HEMATITE (see no.2, p.58): from Greek, *haima*, meaning blood.
Iron oxide; dark grey to black; metallic lustre.
Historical use: Believed to confer invulnerability in battle and achieve a favourable response to any petition. Recommended for blood disorders and protection against excessive blood loss.
Associated words/phrases: Grounding; "stone for the mind"; balances yin-yang; reduces excess body heat; transforms negativity.
Chakras: Base, Throat.

JADE (see no.17, p.63): Name given to two distinct minerals: nephrite from Greek, *nephros* meaning kidney, and jadeite from Spanish, *piedra de ijada,* meaning "stone for the loins", both alluding to the ancient belief that jade could cure kidney stones.
Nephrite: calcium magnesium iron silicate; dark green to cream.
Jadeite: sodium aluminium silicate; range of colours including green, pink, red, blue, black, and orange.
Special note: Nephrite more common than jadeite; sometimes dyed to improve colour.
Historical use: Revered by many civilizations from China to New Zealand. The symbol of the heart in Ancient Egypt and Central America, where a piece of jade was placed in or near the body of dead nobles to symbolize their new heart.
Associated words/phrases: Regulates heart beat; increases vitality; encourages harmony; puts things into perspective; inspires wisdom; prolongs life; protective; aids dream work.
Chakras: Heart, Crown.

LAPIS LAZULI (see no.1, p.58): from Latin, *lapis,* meaning "stone" and Arabic, *azul,* meaning "blue".
Sodium calcium aluminium sulfate silicate; distinctive blue rock with flecks of gold or white from pyrite or calcite inclusions.
Historical use: Said to protect against spirits of darkness as its colour symbolized the heavens. Amulets of lapis lazuli believed to convey protective powers in Ancient Egypt.
Associated words/phrases: Spiritual awakening; mental clarity; protects against depression; aids self-expression; enhances artistic endeavours; encourages expansiveness; boosts immune system.
Chakras: Throat, Third Eye.

MALACHITE (see no.6, p.59): from Greek, *malache,* meaning "mallow leaf".
Copper hydroxycarbonate; always green with characteristic banding.
Historical use: Considered a particularly valuable talisman for children. Would protect wearer from falls and warn them of impending danger by breaking into several pieces.
Associated words/phrases: Soothing; calming; promotes inner peace and compassion; balances physical body; anti-depressant; excellent for meditation and dream work; cleansing; amplifies current mood.
Chakras: Solar plexus, Heart.

MOONSTONE (see no.15, p.62):
Feldspar group (adularia orthoclase); potassium aluminium silicate; opalescent with blue or white sheen, usually colourless, white or silver.
Historical use: If placed in the mouth when the moon is full this stone was believed to help lovers find out what lay in store for them in the future.
Associated words/phrases: Calms emotions; balances oversensitivity; opens up one's feminine side; heightens intuition and receptivity; aids awareness of subconscious feelings; assists hormonal equilibrium during menstrual cycle.
Chakras: Sacral, Heart.

ROCK CRYSTAL (CLEAR QUARTZ) (see no.10, p.59): from Greek, *krystallos,* "ice".
Quartz family; silicon dioxide; colourless, transparent.

Historical use: A popular "fetish" of the Cherokee, who believed it gave them greater power in hunting and divination. Also used to quench thirst in Ancient Greece and Rome, where quartz was believed to be unmeltable ice.
Associated words/phrases: "The Master Crystal"; most versatile of all crystals; symbol of balance and purity; aids meditation; amplifies effects of other crystals (see also pp.50-1).
Chakras: All chakras, particularly Crown.

ROSE QUARTZ (see no.5, p.58):

Quartz family; silicon dioxide; always pink.
Historical use: Symbol of love and beauty. Masks cut from rose quartz were used to beautify skin in Ancient Egypt.
Associated words/phrases: Unconditional love (for ourselves and others); peace; good for children; emotional support; positive; responsive; heightens self-esteem; comforting; releases excess fluids and impurities from the body.
Chakras: Base, Solar plexus, Heart.

SODALITE (see no.7, p.59):

Sodium aluminium silicate; all shades of blue.
Historical use: Not featured in ancient writings. May have been linked with lapis lazuli, which it loosely resembles.
Associated words/phrases: Encourages objectivity and new perspectives; balances metabolism; aids sleep; increases spiritual awareness; prolongs physical endurance; creates harmony between conscious and subconscious; helps you "lighten up".
Chakra: Throat.

TIGER'S EYE (see no.14, p.62):

Chatoyant quartz (iridescent, "cat's eye effect"); silicon dioxide; black to dark brown with fibrous inclusions of yellow and golden-brown stripes.
Special note: Other varieties of chatoyant quartz are cat's eye and hawk's eye.
Historical use: The chatoyant property of tiger's eye was believed to improve eyesight, prevent eye diseases, and avert the "evil eye".
Associated words/phrases: Aids concentration; focuses energy to meet challenges; grounding; symbol of inner strength; encourages optimism; balances yin-yang energy; enhances creativity.
Chakras: Base, Sacral.

TURQUOISE (see no. 16, p.63): from

French, *turquoise,* meaning "Turkish".
Hydrated copper aluminium phosphate; sky blue to green.
Special note: Porous and prone to cracking and fading – may be waxed to prevent this; care needed in the sun.
Historical use: Turquoise was said to darken or lighten to indicate a change in a person's health. This gemstone is greatly affected by alterations in temperature and humidity and also responds to skin secretions like sebum and perspiration.
Associated words/phrases: Clarity of communication; encourages affinity with others; leads to greater self-awareness and "true purpose"; eases rheumatism and arthritis.
Chakra: Throat.

WATERMELON TOURMALINE (see no.13,

p.62): from Sinhalese, *turamali,* meaning "stone attracting ash" (relating to its pyroelectric properties, see p.42).
Complex borosilicate; bi-coloured – green rim, pink centre – or vice versa.
Historical use: Only known since the 18th century.
Associated words/phrases: Regulates hormones and metabolism; "pulls weeds, plants seeds"; helps recovery from "heartache"; helps lighten you up; symbolizes balance.
Chakra: Heart.

TWENTY KEY CRYSTALS (NUMBERS 11 TO 20)

THE SEVEN MAJOR CHAKRAS

Chakras are vortices of energy, which, while anatomically undectable, form part of the ancient Indian explanation for how vital energy is drawn in and channelled through the body. They are traditionally positioned over certain nerve plexes and endocrine centres of the physical body.

◆ SOLAR PLEXUS (MANIPURA)
Position: Below breastbone, behind stomach. Linked to digestive system – pancreas, liver, and stomach.
Associated element: Fire
Qualities: Individuality and psychic awareness. Represents link between mind and emotions, where we process negative feelings, leading to digestive disorders and "butterflies".

◆ SACRAL CHAKRA (SVADISTHANA)
Position: Below navel. Linked with adrenals. Adrenalin released for "fight or flight". If not channelled effectively, contributes to stress.
Associated element: Water.
Qualities: Creativity, sexuality, authority, and power. If you feel ineffective or insecure meditate on this chakra (visualize an orange disc spinning clockwise).

◆ HEART (ANAHATA)
Position: Centre of the chest.
Associated element: Air.
Qualities: Linked to thymus (controls immune system). Seat of "higher" emotions: tenderness, compassion, unconditional love, and universal truth. Energies affect heart, lungs, upper chest and back, and bronchial tubes.

◆ ROOT/BASE CHAKRA (MULADHARA)
Position: Between anus and genitals. Linked with reproductive glands.
Associated element: Earth.
Function: Houses resting "kundalini" or basic, evolutionary life force (coiled serpent), whose goal is to rise through each chakra, until it reaches the crown (enlightenment).
Quality: Synonymous with "grounding" (see p.81) and the physical self.

◆ **CROWN (SAHASRARA)**
Position: On top of the head. Linked with pituitary or pineal gland (pineal produces melatonin, regulating the "internal clock").
Function: Seat of spirituality – René Descartes' (1596-1650) seat of the soul or "ghost in the machine", where body and mind interact.
Qualities: Associated with higher self and enlightenment – perfection of mind, body, and spirit.

◆ **THIRD EYE/BROW (AJNA)**
Position: Above and between eyebrows. Linked to pituitary or pineal gland – opinions vary (see Crown, above).
Associated element: Telepathic energy
Qualities: Seat of spiritual vision, higher intuition, and true wisdom, sometimes called "sixth sense". Physically its energies affect facial nerves, eyes, head, and brain.

◆ **THROAT (VISUDDHA)**
Position: Centrally at base of neck.
Associated element: Ether.
Qualities: Traditionally represents communication and self-expression through thoughts, writing, speech, dance, and art. Traditionally linked with thyroid gland (controls metabolic rate) but also affects throat, ears, nose, mouth, and neck.

4

CRYSTAL CLEAR

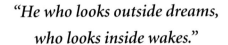

"He who looks outside dreams,
who looks inside wakes."

C.G. JUNG

The mind is a powerful healing tool. Scientists and physicians are at last seriously investigating the link between the mind, emotions, and health. You may recall feeling healthy and energized when falling in love. Such intensity can positively affect the body's functioning. A psychosomatic network of endorphins and neuropeptides is the physiological link between the mind and natural healing response. Many of the receptors for these biochemical transmitters cluster not just in the brain but also in receptor sites associated with emotions.

Does the "mind" exist and, if so, where? We are all aware of intuitions that come "out of the ether". The mind is an unexplained form of energy which does not emanate from the physical body but interacts with it. It is a whisper so soft that the brain's cacophony of thoughts, desires, and sensations regularly drowns it out. If only you could hear your mind's message you could develop inner peace, and promote physical well-being. One way to tap into your mind is to meditate, focusing on one thing, not many. It is about paying attention and developing "present moment awareness". So a single, focused thought can become a powerful tool to harness natural self-healing ability.

This chapter highlights how crystals and meditation can be combined. One way is to use a favourite crystal as a meditative focus. Or, there are creative visualizations. Creating visual images of wholeness and well-being is an essential part of using the crystal healing layouts outlined in Chapter Five.

CRYSTALS AND CHAKRAS

The positioning of the seven major chakras relates to the control of the metabolic, glandular, immune, central nervous systems, and reproductive organs. Each chakra behaves like a self-opening valve filtering the "electrical current" of the Universal Life Force into the body. Think of the chakras as electrical sockets. The moment we push a plug in and switch on we experience electrical power. But if we cut into the wall to try and "find" the electrical current all we find are wires and transformers. We take it on trust that the electrical energy we need will be available. There is still no scientific way of "proving" that vital energy and its channels actually exist – we simply must accept, esoterically, that they do.

The sevenfold major chakra system is the most widely accepted (see below). However, there are minor chakras

Chart notes
◆ *Each chakra – from the root or base upward – is linked to the colours of the rainbow: red, orange, yellow, green, blue, indigo, and violet.*
◆ *Rock crystal (clear quartz) used on any chakra will magnify the power of any crystals placed there.*

THE SEVEN CHAKRAS – AND THEIR CORRESPONDING COLOURS AND CRYSTALS

	ROOT OR BASE (perineum)	SACRAL (below navel)	SOLAR PLEXUS
COLOURS	Red Mauve Brown	Orange Gold Amber	Yellow Gold Rose
ELEMENT	Earth	Water	Fire
SENSE	Smell	Taste	Sight
SELF ASPECT	Physical energy and Vitality	Creativity/ Sexual expression	Personal power/ Fulfilment
CRYSTAL (20 KEY CRYSTALS, SEE PAGES 56-63)	Agate Bloodstone Tiger's eye Hematite	Moonstone Tiger's eye Citrine Carnelian	Citrine Rose quartz Aventurine quartz Malachite
(OTHER SUGGESTIONS)	*Carnelian Rhodochrosite*	*Rutilated quartz Golden topaz*	*Smoky quartz Sunstone*

all over the body creating a dynamic, interlinking energy system. The analogy of a spinning wheel rotated by an external energy force perfectly describes the chakras. Each chakra has a corresponding front and back location point, except for the crown and root (base). The chakras act as both transmitters and transformers of energy. They channel the stream of energy from the Universal Life Force and control the level and speed of energy flowing between each part of the human energy system (see also pp.64-5). For crystal bodywork, in which the crystals are placed on the chakras, choose the right crystals for your needs, cleanse them, and meditate to achieve a peaceful frame of mind. For problems directly corresponding to their physical locations, place the crystal over the appropriate chakra (see pp.114-15).

Chakras, colours, crystals
Colour is a form of energy. The seven chakras are assigned a different colour corresponding to their vibratory rates, but any colour crystal can be used on any chakra as long as their relationship "feels" right. The purpose of placing certain colours on chakras is to balance them, enabling energy channelled through them to vibrate at the correct frequency.

HEART	THROAT	THIRD EYE OR BROW	CROWN (top of head)
Green	Blue	Indigo	Violet
Pink	Silver	Mauve	Gold
	Turquoise	Turquoise	White
Air	Ether	Telepathic energy	Cosmic energy
Touch	Hearing	Sixth sense	Seventh sense
Compassion/ Humanitarianism	Communication/ Self-expression	Higher intuition/ Psychic powers	Transmutation
Jade	Aquamarine	Amethyst	Amethyst
Aventurine quartz	Lapis lazuli	Fluorite	Celestite
Watermelon tourmaline	Turquoise	Lapis lazuli	Jade
Rose quartz	Celestite	Sodalite	Rock crystal (clear quartz)
Emerald	*Blue-laced agate*	*Purple apatite*	*Diamond*
Sugilite	*Aqua aura*	*Azurite*	*Gold calcite*

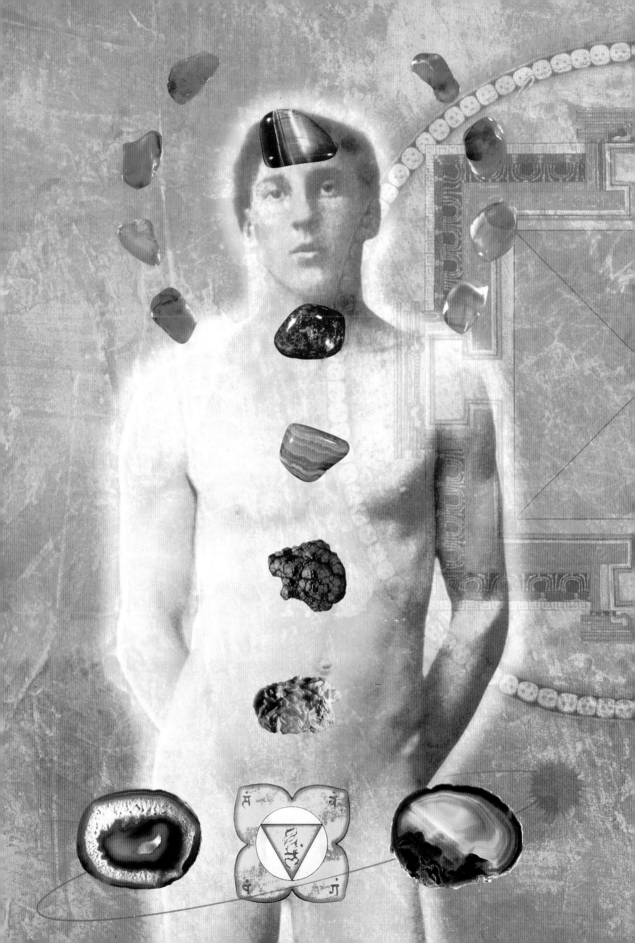

The
Root or Base Chakra
*Red, Earth, Smell,
Physical energy and Vitality*

◆

CORRESPONDING CRYSTALS

*Agate, Bloodstone, Tiger's eye,
Hematite, Carnelian,
Rhodochrosite*

(See also p.68)

◆

QUESTIONS ABOUT MEDITATION

◆ **What can I expect from meditating?**
Try not to pre-empt, judge, or influence your medita-
tions. You are unique and so are your experiences.
Accept what happens, without evaluating or judging.

◆ **Is meditation anything to do with religion?**
Many religions and philosophies incorporate meditation, but you don't need to belong to one to
participate.

◆ **How does meditation affect the physical body?**
Meditation produces physiological shifts. Blood pressure, cholesterol, respiration, and stress hormone levels are lowered. There is an upsurge of energy and
increased endorphin levels, plus a slowing of
brainwave activity.

◆ **How does meditation "heal"?**
By releasing or preventing stress; by stimulating the
body to function more efficiently; by allowing us to
hear that "still, small voice" which can guide us to
develop a new perspective on challenges.

◆ **Supposing I have trouble sitting still and relaxing?**
Then you are a perfect candidate for meditation.
Select an undemanding time of day and don't set
unrealistic targets. Start with five minutes twice a day
and build up gradually. Calm down with breathing
exercises (see p.80).

◆ **How long should I meditate each day?**
Quality is more important than quantity. Five or ten
minutes' focused thought is more beneficial than
hours of drifting. Try to meditate once or twice a day.
The important thing is not length of time spent but
how regularly you meditate and how much you apply
the benefits to everyday life. These include enhanced
relaxation, taking a different perspective on life, and
accessing the answers to troubling problems.

*The effects of meditation
on the brain*
*Imagine the brain as a
powerful yet stationary car
revving its engine so loudly
that the whispering "mind"
in the back seat cannot be
heard. As our meditative
journey progresses the
brain changes its levels of
output – similar to changing gear – until it reaches a
low-level "purring". A
peaceful, external environment combined with
internal calm shifts your
brainwaves into different
levels of consciousness.*

Readiness for crystal healing
*Once you have gained a
certain mastery of meditation
and visualization you will be
ready to engage in crystal self-
healing. Don't worry if you are
still sceptical. The very fact
that you are reading this book
implies that, subconsciously,
you believe that it is relevant.
This belief, and the emotion
created when you lovingly
work with crystals, harness the
vibrational energy that stimu-
lates your body's self-healing
ability. Chapter Five outlines
exactly how you can bring this
about.*

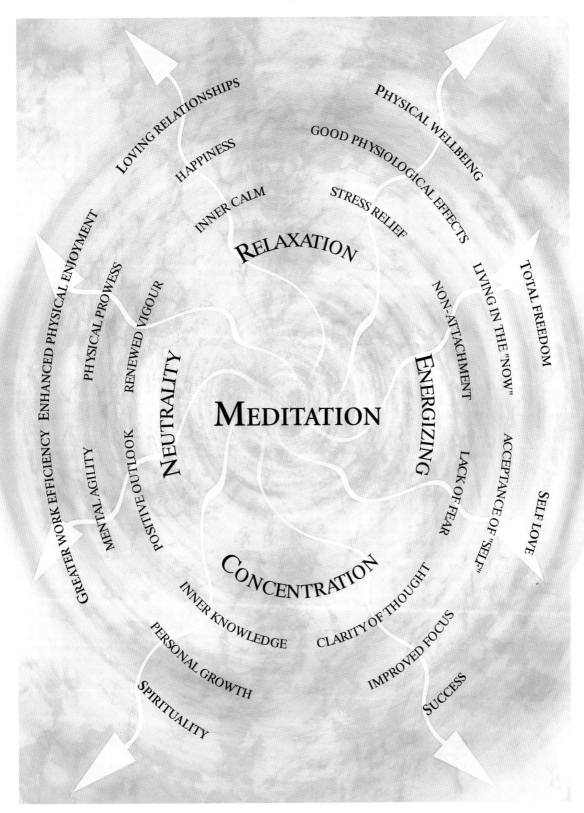

The
Sacral Chakra
Orange, Water, Taste,
Creativity/Sexual expression

◆

CORRESPONDING CRYSTALS

Moonstone, Tiger's eye, Citrine,
Carnelian, Rutilated quartz,
Golden topaz

(See also p.68)

◆

LEVELS OF CONSCIOUSNESS

During meditation the level of electrical activity in the brain's cerebral cortex changes. With the advent of electroencephalograms (EEGs) in the 1960s it has been possible to measure the electrical activity of the brain. Researchers found that different "states", such as sleep and meditation, produced different levels of electrical activity. These "brain states" are measured in hertz (Hz) or cycles per second (cps).

BRAIN STATES

◆ BETA STATE: Under normal levels of awareness the brain's pulse rate averages 20 Hz (cps). Thoughts drown out intuitive messages. Attention is focused externally.

◆ ALPHA STATE: Averaging 7.8-14 Hz (cps), this state occurs just before sleep and on waking, when creative ideas may occur. This is the "gear" the brain slips into during creative visualization (see p.88). Attention is divided between external and internal.

◆ THETA STATE: The electrical activity of the brain operates at around 3.2-7.8 Hz (cps).

This state of enhanced focus is the true meditative state, bringing about "peak experiences" including sudden ecstasy, a sense of wonder and delight, a feeling of understanding life plus a sense of "belonging". Dreaming, trance, and hypnosis are typical states.

◆ DELTA STATE: The lowest-known level of brain activity – pulse rate slows to 0.1-3.2 Hz (cps). These patterns are only accomplished while awake by experienced meditators and mystics. They cause a different perception and information processing capacity normally only achieved during deep sleep, unconsciousness, or coma.

THE PLATONIC SOLIDS
The Ancient Greeks regularly meditated by visualizing five three-dimensional, geometric shapes known as the Platonic Solids. They believed they could alter their consciousness and achieve mystical experiences. The five shapes – tetrahedron, cube, octahedron, dodecahedron, and icosahedron – all occur naturally in crystals.

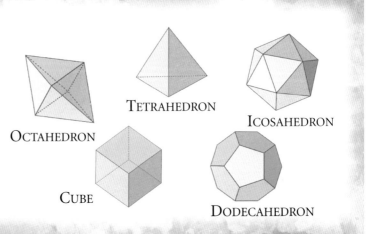

OCTAHEDRON

TETRAHEDRON

ICOSAHEDRON

CUBE

DODECAHEDRON

PREPARATION FOR MEDITATION

A FEW QUESTIONS BEFORE YOU START:

◆ Is your meditation room spacious enough for you to move about in or lie outstretched?

◆ Is it a room you really like, in which you feel comfortable?

◆ Do you feel secure? Can you lock the door?

◆ Is the ventilation good?

◆ Will you be warm and comfortable enough? What about a rug or cushions?

◆ Do you have enough time? Choose early morning or the evening, when you have no pressing appointments afterwards.

◆ Will the telephone disturb you? What about a "do not disturb" sign on your door?

◆ Do your clothes feel too restrictive?

◆ If you decide to burn incense, do you really like the smell? Place some water in the room so the atmosphere doesn't become too dry.

◆ What position will you feel most comfortable in – lying down, sitting in a chair, or on the floor?

◆ Will your position send you to sleep?

◆ Are you in the right frame of mind? If you feel tense, try free-form movement to physically "shake off" negative feelings before starting.

◆ Do you have a glass of water to hand to drink directly afterwards? This will help rehydrate and ground you (see p.81).

◆ Correct breathing is important in meditation. Do you need to clear your nose? Keep some tissues to hand.

◆ If you are playing a music or guided meditation tape, is your tape recorder within easy reach?

◆ Is the music you have chosen suitable? Relaxing nature sounds work best.

◆ Have your meditation crystals been cleansed and tuned? If not, see pp.52-5.

◆ Finally – and perhaps most importantly – have you been to the toilet/bathroom?

◆

The
Solar Plexus Chakra
*Yellow, Fire, Sight,
Personal power/Fulfilment*

❖

CORRESPONDING CRYSTALS

*Citrine, Rose quartz,
Aventurine quartz, Malachite,
Smoky quartz, Sunstone*

(See also p.68)

❖

FOUR STEPS TO SUCCESSFUL MEDITATING

Deep meditation involves opening your mind to new levels of consciousness, resulting in enhanced creativity and intuition. Creative visualization (or guided meditation) is useful when you want to focus on a particular problem or stimulate your body's innate healing response.

Emotions play a fundamental part in healing mental anguish and physical symptoms. Therefore the crystals you choose should be special to you. Most of us "love" an inanimate object; try to engender that depth of feeling.

Quartz crystal is traditionally the favoured choice for meditation as it is believed to represent the connection between mind and body. Amethyst and rock crystal (clear quartz) are two excellent choices. Amethyst is the "stone of meditation", creating a state of enhanced spirituality and contentment. Rock crystal (clear quartz) represents the clarity of mind that you aim to achieve through meditation. Its "inclusions" are particularly valuable for stimulating the imagination during visualization (see pp.92-3). You may find it helpful to record these instructions on tape (see p.89).

1. THE BREATH

Slow breathing calms the mind. Breathing directly influences the body's nervous system. Poor breathing reduces oxygen intake and impairs metabolism. Think about your breathing and how much you fill your lungs. Before meditating, centre yourself with the retention breathing exercise (see right). Centring is a state of calm receptivity. Observing the breath is the most basic yet powerful form of meditation, focusing attention away from the chatter of thoughts. Try placing the tip of your tongue on the alveolar ridge (behind the front teeth). This closes the body's energy circuit, retaining more "prana", or life force.

The retention breathing exercise

◆ *Place the tip of your tongue on the alveolar ridge (behind the front teeth). Try to keep it there.*

◆ *Exhale fully and audibly through the mouth.*

◆ *Close the mouth and inhale quietly through the nose to a count of three.*

◆ *Hold the breath to a count of twelve. Exhale audibly through the mouth for a count of six. Repeat four times. Then try to increase the initial inhalation to a four- or five-second breath, keeping a ratio of:*
1 (inhalation)
4 (retention)
2 (exhalation).

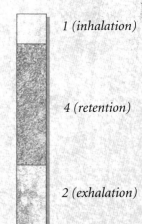

1 (inhalation)

4 (retention)

2 (exhalation)

2. THE POSITION

Sit upright with spine straight, placing cushions under your feet or knees. During crystal healing, when stones are placed on the body, it is necessary to lie down. However, during normal meditation, try to avoid lying as you may fall asleep. Rest your hands comfortably on your upper thighs with palms upward, or with the fingers linked at the navel.

3. VISUAL FOCUS

Hold the crystal before meditating. Place a larger crystal on a table or floor in front of you. Half-close the eyes and gaze at it with "soft focus". Keeping the eyes partly closed reduces distractions picked up by peripheral vision and you are less likely to fall asleep. Looking slightly downward usually feels more comfortable.

4. GROUNDING

Successful meditation, when your brain completely slows down, can leave you light-headed. Start your session by grounding yourself by imagining that your feet (or body if lying) are connected with the earth. Visualize your feet as deeply buried tree roots. Place a small piece of hematite in each sock, or wear smoky quartz to help you stay grounded during meditation. Afterwards, let your brain come back up to speed again (see right).

Ways of grounding
Do one or more of the following directly after meditating to bring yourself back to normal consciousness:
◆ *Drink a glass of water.*
◆ *Rub your hands together briskly.*
◆ *Walk barefoot on the ground outside.*
◆ *Wiggle your toes.*

The
Heart Chakra
Green, Air, Touch,
Compassion/Humanitarianism

◆

CORRESPONDING CRYSTALS

Jade, Aventurine quartz
Watermelon tourmaline,
Rose quartz, Emerald, Sugilite

(See also p.69)

◆

CRYSTAL FOCUS MEDITATION

This is an ideal stress-relieving or self-development exercise. Use it while keeping a dream diary to help you gain an insight into your dreams. Maintaining your focus on a crystal helps quieten chatter in your head, enabling you to tap into new levels of awareness. You then start to become a human "being" instead of merely a "doing".

1. Run through the meditation preparation checklist (see p.77).

2. Choose a crystal cleansed, dedicated, and tuned for meditation (see pp 52-5) and hold it, or place it before you. Or take three similar crystals and position them in an equilateral triangle big enough to sit within (a highly charged energy field).

3. Sit on a chair with feet flat on the floor or sit on the ground. Ensure that you are comfortable and that your spine is straight.

4. Centre yourself with the retention breathing exercise on page 80.

5. Half-close your eyes and gaze at the crystal.

6. Concentrate on its colour, shape, and size, but do not try to make sense of, or "analyse", what you see.

7. Breathe deeply and slowly.

8. Whenever an unconnected thought comes, let it float
away like a cloud and re-direct attention back to the crystal.

9. Don't battle with your thoughts...Just acknowledge them and let them go...

10. Thoughts are natural and can never be eliminated...
But remember that you are more than your thoughts,
your emotions, or your feelings...

11. You are more than any aches, pains, or disease...

12. As you continue to breathe slowly and deeply, resting your
gaze on your crystal, allow yourself to open up to higher levels of
consciousness...

13. Without expectation, without judgement, and
without trying to influence the experience, open
your mind to the Universal Life Force. (Spend the
next 5-10 minutes in silent meditation.)

14. Now you are ready to come out of meditation. Take several deep breaths. Continue to focus on the crystal but open
your eyes gradually. Colours may be enhanced, the edges of
objects sharper, and you may have temporarily lost all sense
of time. These are natural "side-effects" of meditation.

15. Take another deep breath and "ground" yourself (see p.81).

◆

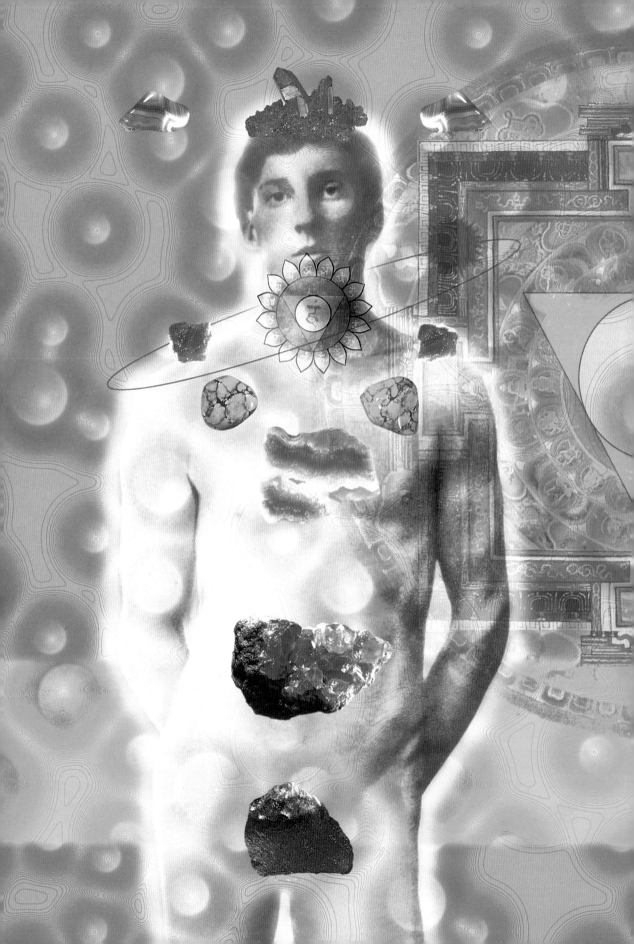

The
Throat Chakra
Blue, Ether, Hearing,
Communication/Self-expression

◆

CORRESPONDING CRYSTALS

Aquamarine, Lapis lazuli,
Turquoise, Celestite, Blue-laced
agate, Aqua aura

(See also p.69)

◆

CREATIVE VISUALIZATION

Being disciplined enough to engage in regular visualization exercises is considered to be the major difference between those who succeed in life and those who merely participate. Many top athletes and businesspeople achieve success through visualizing. Linford Christie closed his eyes and is believed to have "seen" himself over the winning line ahead of the field when he won the 100 metres sprint in the 1992 Olympic Games.

A large part of the brain's cerebral cortex is concerned with processing information from the eyes. When it becomes disengaged from that task, for example during meditation, its attention turns inward. In this mode the cerebral cortex becomes a vital channel for mind/body communication.

The brain cannot tell the difference between what is real and what is realistically imagined. That is why visualizing is so powerful. Feeling, hearing, tasting, touching, and smelling an imaginary experience is, as far as your brain is concerned, as good as "reality". As with other forms of meditation, regular practice is vital. Visualizing should not take any longer than ten or fifteen minutes, but for effects to manifest themselves quickly you should aim to repeat the suggested exercises at least once a day, preferably just before bedtime. You can also write your own guided meditations. Ensure they contain the key ingredients picked out in the panel below.

The six steps of visualization
1. Ask yourself whether you want to heal your body, feel better about yourself, create new opportunities in life.
2. Relax your body and mind as you do when meditating (see pp.80-1).
3. Visualize your chosen outcome in as much detail as possible, employing all your senses.
4. "Ground" yourself and make an affirmatory statement that reinforces that positive outcome (see p.81).
5. Continue to act as if that positive outcome has already taken place.
6. Act on any hunches or intuitions which will help achieve your new reality.

THE KEY INGREDIENTS OF VISUALIZATION

◆ Dynamic action. See yourself on a journey, perhaps travelling along a road.

◆ Engage all the senses. During your journey remind yourself to look, feel, taste, touch, or smell everything. Colour is particularly important. Introduce the relevant shades into your journey.

◆ Engender emotion – the stronger the better (important for physical healing). The images you conjure should therefore be important to you, which you relate to strongly, producing an emotional response.

PREPARING YOUR OWN TAPES

It is often a good idea to make your own tapes. The advantage is that they can be totally personalized. The suggested texts in this chapter can be changed to suit you and then recorded on to blank cassettes. Here are a few guidelines:

◆ Consider whether you might prefer someone else to record their voice.
◆ Think carefully about background music.
◆ Speak slowly and clearly. Change the text before you actually start recording.
◆ Leave enough time between each instruction to carry it out.
◆ When you have covered all the preparatory instructions, leave the tape running for the time you want the period of silence to last.
◆ Lead into your closing, grounding instructions gently so that you do not give yourself a sudden jolt upon hearing a voice after a period of silence.

The lemon test
Try this simple exercise. It shows how thoughts affect experience. Close your eyes and imagine you are holding a lemon. "See" its thick yellowy-green skin. Feel the pitted texture. Smell that fresh, clean aroma. In your mind's eye watch how you break into the flesh with your fingers so that the juices flow over your hands. Taste the bitterness. Are you salivating yet?

AFFIRMATIONS

These are positive statements that reinforce your visualizations. They need to be worded correctly to be effective. Your mind – consciously or subconsciously – will not accept something that is patently untrue.

◆ Always begin with the words "I am".
◆ Follow with a verb that implies development, i.e. you know you haven't achieved your goal yet, but you are working on it.
◆ State the desired outcome.

Examples:

◆ "I am becoming a confident public speaker."
◆ "I am beginning to lose weight."

The
Third eye or
Brow Chakra
*Indigo, Telepathic energy, Sixth sense,
Higher intuition/Psychic powers*

◆

CORRESPONDING CRYSTALS

*Amethyst, Fluorite, Lapis lazuli,
Sodalite, Purple apatite, Azurite*

(See also p.69)

◆

PROBLEM-SOLVING VISUALIZATION

Use this guided meditation whenever you have a question or problem for which your conscious mind is unable to provide an answer. The dots between each sentence indicate a suitable pause. Follow steps 1-7 of the meditation on page 84 before you commence. Focus your concentration on the crystal in front of you.

 Remain aware of the thoughts and feelings you experienced during this merging meditation. Remind yourself that you can tune in to these feelings and thoughts any time you want. You can also go back into that private place any time you feel you need to, to ask a question and receive the answer. Reinforce your visualization with the appropriate affirmation.

1. Close your eyes, allowing the crystal to remain in your "mind's eye". The more often you do this exercise the more readily you will "see" the crystal, even if you do not consider yourself to be a natural "visualizer".

2. Allow this image of the crystal to grow larger and larger until it completely envelops your whole being…

3. Imagine that you are at the heart of the crystal…

4. Everything is blurring and soon you can no longer discern where your body ends and the crystal begins…

5. Be aware that your physical form and consciousness have become one with the crystal…

6. Contemplate for a moment how it feels to share the same perfection, the same order, the same clarity as your crystal…

Focus on the sensations which this realization produces…

7. You are as unique and perfect as the crystal…

It forms a protective shield around you so that you are totally safe and secure. Try to allow all extraneous thoughts to float through your mind like wispy clouds. It is perfectly natural to have thoughts. . . but you are their controller – not the other way around…

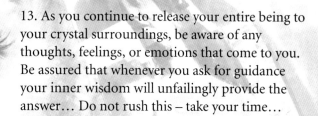

14. When you sense your inner journey is completed it is time to bring about your separation from the crystal. Imagine you have an inner "contrast" switch that sharpens and defines your external shape and, at the same time, reduces the crystal to its normal size…Fade this mental picture from your mind, open your eyes and take a few deep breaths or wiggle your toes to "ground" yourself.

13. As you continue to release your entire being to your crystal surroundings, be aware of any thoughts, feelings, or emotions that come to you. Be assured that whenever you ask for guidance your inner wisdom will unfailingly provide the answer… Do not rush this – take your time…

12. Know that deep within you there is a fount of all knowledge whose whispered wisdom you can only access when the everyday cacophony of your heart and mind has been subdued… There is nothing you can not know – from the past, the present, or the future.

11. Is everything quiet or can you detect certain sounds? Just acknowledge them and let them go. Take a few, deep breaths and explore this new sensation of utter, inner peace. When you feel completely quiet, bring to mind the question or problem that has been troubling you…

10. Is it warm or cool? What does it smell like here, in your crystal kingdom? Consider whether you sense light or shadows…

9. Now bring your focus back to what it is like to be part of this crystal world. Be aware of the surrounding temperature…

8. When thoughts come into your head, acknowledge them and let them drift away as if they were passing acquaintances…one moment there, another – gone.

◆

The
Crown Chakra
Violet, Cosmic energy,
Seventh sense, Transmutation

— ◆ —

Corresponding Crystals

Amethyst, Celestite, Jade,
Rock crystal (clear quartz),
Diamond, Gold calcite

(See also p.69)

— ◆ —

A CHILD'S VISUALIZATION

This is a pro-active way of introducing the notion of self-healing for a child's emotional or physical problems. Ask the child to choose and hold a favourite crystal that is cleansed, dedicated, and tuned for meditation purposes (see pp.52-5). Ensure that he or she is warm and comfortable. Read the following script slowly and clearly. Remind the child that he or she does not need to "do" anything. Everything takes place in the imagination.

You can change the imagery to suit the age and sex of the child. Amend the text also to suit changing circumstances, for example, courage to overcome fears, easing of aches and pains, or bringing about happier relationships. Remember to pre-prepare a positive statement that the child can say aloud at the end of the visualization. (The dots indicate a suitable pause.)

1. Close your eyes and imagine you are standing on a golden road that stretches far into the distance…

You are walking along this road, holding your favourite crystal…
The sun is shining and you can feel the warmth of it on your skin…
There is a gentle breeze and under your feet you can feel the thick grassy carpet…

2. As you walk farther along this road you can see a great big, crystal mountain…
It is the same colour and shape as your own favourite crystal…

Behind the mountain is a beautiful rainbow…

As you get closer you can see the rainbow's colours shining on the mountain, creating layers of different colours.…

3. See each of the colours in turn – red, orange, yellow, green, blue, purple, and gold. The mountain knows you are its friend and is happy to let you climb on its back…But first you need to be a little lighter…

4. The mountain asks you to leave all your worries, fears, or sadness at the bottom…

5. They make you too heavy to climb up the mountain…Take off your worries, fears, or sadness as if you were taking off a heavy, uncomfortable bag…

6. Leave them on the ground at the bottom of the mountain now…

…and start to climb…

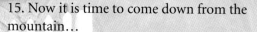

15. Now it is time to come down from the mountain…

16. Silently thank the mountain for your magic wish…

14. What do you wish for? (Perhaps suggest a happy solution to whatever is troubling the child.)

13. The magic well is asking you to make a wish…

17. Perhaps you feel like skipping or running or just walking…

12. Hear the splash as the coin hits the water.

11. Throw it into the well…

18. But before you know it you are back again on the golden road and coming home.

10. Feel in your pocket and pull out the golden coin that is in there…

19. Open your eyes and give yourself a big stretch and a smile.

9. The fence is high enough to protect you but low enough for you to look down into the sparkling, blue water…

20. Rub your hands together as fast as you can…

8. You are nearly at the top, where ahead there is a magic well with a fence around it…

21. Take a big breath and blow out any worries or fears or sadness that you forgot to leave behind…

7. The road slopes very gently and you have lots of energy as you march up to the top of the mountain…

22. What you have imagined is your own, special place, somewhere only you can go…

And you can go there again, whenever you like.

5

CRYSTAL HEALING

— ◆ —

*"Energy medicine is capable of accomplishing
with a minimum of effort what chemical and
physical treatments can only do very clumsily."*

LESLIE KENTON, PASSAGE TO POWER

The oldest-known systems of health were developed in India
and China around 4000 years ago. While different therapies and
exercises emerged from them – for example, acupuncture,
reflexology, qigong, and meditation – the underlying principle
is the same, that an elaborate, vital energy system animates all
living things. This life force, known in Ancient Chinese
medicine as "chi", flows through channels called meridians. Any
impediment to the free flow of this life energy is considered to
be the main cause of dis-ease. Chi is like the dynamic force of
water flowing through a hose; a blockage restricts flow. Not only
does the power of the water become weak but it also strains
other parts of the system.

The Ancient Chinese also recognized two opposing but complementary forces at work in all things – the concept of polarity
known as "yin" and "yang". Yin energies are receptive, calming,
feminine, and negative, while yang is directive, energizing, mas-
culine, and positive. An imbalance of either causes a wide range
of health problems.

Crystal healing embraces this ancient wisdom. Using crystals
is a form of vibrational healing or "energy medicine" and crystals are tools to help you balance this vital life force and bring
about optimum health. The crystal healing layouts (see pp.106-
111), in the form of case studies, outline some different uses for
single-terminated quartz crystals plus a selection of other commonly used crystals.

AMETHYST

— ◆ —

THE HUMAN ENERGY FIELD

Early civilizations intuitively knew about the subtle energy system coursing through all life. Their quieter world
and closeness to nature nurtured the sensitivity required
to respond to a spiritual as well as a physical presence.
Today the most enlightened scientists and physicians
validate subtle energy using space-age technology but
talk about it in terms of electromagnetic fields.

THE AURA

The phenomenon known esoterically as the "aura" is the
body's bio-electromagnetic field, with "bio" meaning life,
"electro" referring to the energy system or electricity that
courses through everything, and "magnetic" relating to
the natural polarities, or the positive and negative aspects
of life.

    From the late 1930s Semyon Kirlian developed a
means of photographing the auric fields of plants,
animals, and humans. His technique involved applying a
low current of high-frequency, high-voltage electric
charge to an aluminium plate resting on a sheet of glass
and photosensitive film. An object – a hand, for example
– was placed on the plate and a photograph taken which
showed the complete auric outline. Plants showed
definite signs of auric imbalance well before they became
visibly diseased. This demonstrated that the condition of
the aura is directly related to future health.

    In esoteric terms the aura is a resonating energy field
of luminous coloured light that penetrates and radiates
out of the physical body from between a few centimetres/
inches to a metre/yard or more. The aura appears in
paintings, artefacts, and sculptures spanning the aborig-
ines of Australia to the Native Americans. Western
religious paintings show the aura as a halo of bright light
around the head or entire body. There may be several
reasons why the vast majority of us cannot see auras. It
appears to be less a case of our physical bodies not being
equipped to detect these particular frequencies, more a
case of not practising hard enough. It seems that we must

Kirlian photograph
Hands are commonly
used, showing the
complete auric outline.
This example shows a
clear outline, indicating
that the person is a good
communicator who gets
on well with people, is
creative, with a clear
sense of self.

◆ ───

intellectually believe that an auric phenomenon exists before we can see it.

That the aura exists is no longer in question. Pioneering research spanning 25 years, led by American neurophysiologist and psychologist Dr Valerie V. Hunt, has scientifically verified this phenomenon long known to ancient Eastern wisdom.

The aura is commonly conceptualized as a series of energy field layers enveloping the physical body like a nest of Russian dolls. This analogy is now considered misleading since it implies not a unified field but one that is segmented. The only difference between the tradition-ally labelled etheric, astral, mental, and spiritual bodies which emanate from each of us is their frequency of vibration. There is no boundary at which one field ends and the others begin as inferred by this imagery.

One of the energy field layers is known as the etheric body. This is the energy template of our physical body and extends just a short distance beyond our physical outline. Changes in this etheric field affect our physical health and emotional state. It is at this level that crystal healing works, in helping to balance and harmonize the energy of the etheric body in order to enhance our total wellbeing.

Healers have long believed that the aura contains information about the physical, mental, spiritual, and emotional state of an individual as well as acting as a pro-tective zone around us. Think of it rather like the infor-mation stored on magnetic tape. Experts in the field of "energy medicine" confirm the predictive role of the aura, based on new research into electromagnetic fields. They say that the aura will play an increasingly important role in preventing disease in the future since dis-eased states show up in the body's energy fields sometimes years before they have a physical impact. Maintaining a healthy aura is truly preventative medicine. This can be achieved in a variety of ways. By surrounding your envi-ronment with healthy plants, visiting naturally energizing places such as mountains, eating fresh produce instead of

Luminous light
Energy radiates from the physical body, which we are capable of seeing as coloured light, or the "aura".

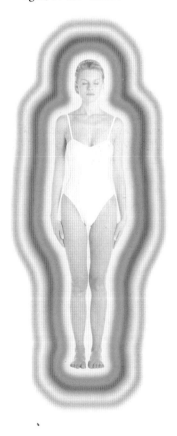

processed foods, and choosing to be with people who do not drain your energy with their negative outlook on life. As you might expect, it also means cutting out toxins such as tobacco.

Unfortunately orthodox medicine continues erroneously to view the human body purely in terms of biochemistry, hence the obsession with treating illness with chemical drugs. That is rather like using a bulldozer to move something for which a gentle nudge would suffice. We have had to wait for technology to catch up with the intuitive knowledge of ancient healers. We now appreciate that there is a level of control within the body that is deeper and more fundamental to health than the biochemical level. The means of accessing this deeper level of control comes from working with the energy centres known as chakras (see also pp.64-5 and 68-9).

Healing hands
Try the following exercise: hold your hands body-width apart, with palms facing. Close your eyes and relax, breathe deeply and allow your shoulders to drop. Slowly bring your hands together. Explore any sensations. You may detect a slight resistance – this is your subtle energy field. Crystals also have energy fields. Experiment with your favourite crystals to see how readily you can detect their electromagnetic energy.

BEFORE AND AFTER CRYSTAL HEALING SESSIONS

◆ Engage your mind while placing the crystals. Which visualization images would be most inspiring for you?

◆ Clear the room of discharged negative energy after a session, using the same cleansing method as you used before (see pp.52-3).

◆ Wash your hands in cool, running water directly afterwards to boost your body's beneficial negative ions.

◆ Re-cleanse your crystals straight after a session. It is easier to remember which crystals you have used and ensures you don't forget this essential process altogether.

BALANCING THE CHAKRAS

For healing to take place the chakras must be balanced and
in harmony. Use two single-terminated quartz crystals.

◆ Lie down and settle yourself comfortably.
◆ Place one of the crystals at your feet, with point toward
   your head. Put the other at the crown of your head with
   the terminated end pointing down.
◆ Take a few minutes to visualize your entire subtle energy
   system becoming harmonized and balanced.
◆ Be aware of any sensations of blockage or soreness.
◆ Ask your higher mind to indicate what the problem is and
   how to deal with it. Act on that intuitive guidance in a
   separate session with whichever additional crystals you
   need to use at that time.

EXERCISES FOR EVERYDAY NEEDS

The body layouts featured in the case studies on the following pages are intended to give you a "taste" of crystal layouts. Try them and if they work for you, that is all the validation you need. You may then decide to engage in extra training. Given that crystal healing is an intuitive process it is impossible to offer layouts to meet every need. This is best achieved through crystal workshops, in which you can explore the different ways your body can benefit from crystal placements (see p.121).

THE ROLE OF CRYSTALS IN HEALING

Every animal, plant, and mineral has an aura or electromagnetic field. This enables organic beings and inorganic objects (such as crystals) to communicate and interact as part of a single, unified energy system. Our personal fields regulate the exchange of energy we have with our environment and others. During a healing session, for example, there is a constant interplay and exchange of energy between the fields of healer and healee. The weak or "sick" field receives energy from the stronger one until the two find their own balance and resonate in harmony.

The principle behind crystal healing is resonance (see also pp.22-4). When a tuning fork, tuned to a particular note, is sounded near a musical instrument, those waves of sound energy are attracted to and overlap a matching form. Strings tuned to the same note resonate while the others remain unaffected. Crystal atoms vibrate when powered by the energy of strong intention. However, there is currently no explanation for crystal healing that sits within the parameters of conventional science.

HEALER OR HEALEE?

The questions (far right) will help you decide how to practice crystal healing. Should you undertake your own crystal healing or approach a healer specializing in crystal work? Each one of us has the inherent ability to heal ourselves. Most of us know what to do with a hammer and

Experiencing the power
As Jung says, "we may never finally know" exactly how or why crystal healing works. Why not experience the power of crystal healing for yourself and let that be all the validation you need?

nails, but that does not make us cabinet makers. The same is true of healing. Not everyone is adept at it and working with a healer can often be valuable and a catalyst for self-healing empowerment.

FINDING THE RIGHT HEALER FOR YOU

In the same way that choosing your crystals is largely intuitive, so is choosing a crystal healer. Finding the right therapist is important. Placing crystals on your body and re-arranging them while maintaining a meditative state is a true challenge. The layouts shown in this chapter are practical for a single individual working on themselves and cover everyday conditions and concerns. They involve using just a few crystals. On pages 64-5 and 68-9 there are also full guidelines and a chart outlining suggested crystals for each of the seven chakras and the conditions for which these are suitable. These will assist you in carrying out a full body layout.

Many crystal healing organizations or individual crystal healers run courses at which you can become adept at crystal placement. However, you are the architect of your own "design for living". Crystals are tools with which you can bring about enhanced wellbeing. You are the one with the power, not the crystal.

The general use of crystals for self-healing is not dangerous. Simply follow the cleansing and tuning processes (see pp.52-5) to ensure that any stored, negative energies from the crystal do not affect your future work. Do not leave your crystals on the chakras for more than five minutes at a time. Crystals, powered by the energy of strong intention, focus and amplify the Universal Life Force being directed into your physical self. Your aim is to kick-start your own healing process, not overwhelm it.

Trust that you will intuitively know how to best use your crystals for your needs. Don't be afraid to experiment. If a crystal placed on a chakra does not feel right, then move it to wherever feels comfortable. By guided by your own intuition – take charge!

Meditate on the following
- ◆ *Do you accept responsibility for your health?*
- ◆ *Do you believe in your natural self-healing ability?*
- ◆ *Do you believe your energy field holds all the information you need for optimum health?*
- ◆ *Do you accept that feeling energized and being filled with love and peace are yours for the asking?*
- ◆ *Have you established a strong connection with your crystals?*
- ◆ *Do you really believe that crystal healing can work for you by yourself?*
- ◆ *Do you have the will-power to set aside time daily?*
- ◆ *Are you prepared to make certain changes in your lifestyle ?*
- ◆ *Do you enjoy pampering yourself at home ?*
- ◆ *Do you learn easily from books?*

If you have answered no to even a few of these questions then you should consider finding a crystal healer who can educate and inspire you.

EIGHT CRYSTAL CASE STUDIES

COPING WITH DEPRESSION

Beth, a bereavement counsellor, could not cope with the distress of one of her clients and was unable to distance herself from his deep depression. A crystal healer helped her select a number of crystals which she kept with her during counselling.

◆ A deep amethyst provided Beth with wisdom, understanding, and the added "depth" she needed to be of the greatest help to her client.
◆ A gentle green aventurine helped her to release negative energy.
◆ Hematite and red jasper were included to ground her, and blue-laced agate offered a focus for emotional release.

Whenever Beth felt agitated during sessions she turned the stones over in her pocket and was reassured by their presence.

DEALING WITH THE SUPPRESSION OF HURT

Tim experienced pain from scar tissue around his colon.
The healer concluded that this was connected with an
inability to confront painful family memories.

- ◆ A gold tiger's eye was placed over the
  solar plexus, stemming the excessive
  discharge of energy from that area.
  This energy loss caused an imbalance
  within Tim's subtle energy, creating
  digestive problems.
- ◆ Blue-laced agate on the throat chakra
  allowed Tim to vocalize and balance his
  emotions.
- ◆ Lapis lazuli over the third eye helped
  him "see" exactly what it was he needed to express.
- ◆ Six double-terminated quartz crystals
  along the line of the colon with energy
  points facing the anus encouraged negative energy to move down and out of
  Tim's body.

A guided visualization, reviewing a
disturbing scene from childhood,
encouraged Tim to release suppressed
hurt. After several treatments the discom-
fort had gone.

A REVITALIZING ENERGY BOOST

Sam had a hectic job as a teacher and needed
regular energy pick-me-ups.

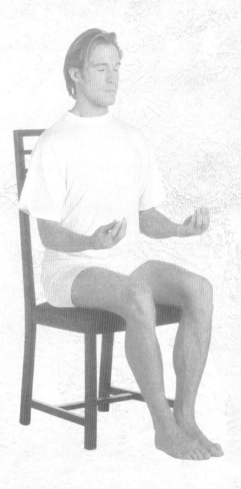

◆ Sam held two single-terminated quartz crystals
   (rock crystal or clear quartz), one in each hand,
   while sitting upright on a chair with feet firmly
   grounded. Terminated (pointed) ends were
   pointed toward his body. This positive polarity
   directed energy from the universal field, distrib-
   uting it throughout the subtle energy system.
◆ Sam breathed slowly and deeply, visualizing the
   energy coursing through his body, leaving him
   feeling revitalized.

WELCOME STRESS RELIEF

Phil tended to become very stressed in his role as
an advertising account executive.

◆ Phil lay comfortably on the floor and placed a
   single-terminated quartz crystal across his
   solar plexus chakra.
◆ He visualized the excess inappropriate energy
   being drawn out of his field and discharged
   into the universal field.

It is important to clear the room of dispersed
negative energy after such a session.

RELIEF FROM HEADACHES

Jo suffered from regular bad headaches.

◈ Rose quartz or aventurine or other gently coloured massive forms of crystal, were placed on or around the affected area for up to five minutes.
◈ Jo was asked to create whatever gentle visualization image she felt was right.
◈ For sharp headaches she held the crystals against the temples. For duller headaches, she lay with her head on a soft pillow and placed a crystal at the back of the head at the point where the base of the skull meets the neck.

HELPING LOCALIZED PAIN RELIEF

Sarah experienced mild arthritis.
This technique can also be used for a sprained muscle, period pain, or rheumatism.

◈ One single-terminated quartz crystal, with the directive, terminated end placed over the painful area, was held in place for a few minutes while Sarah visualized a soothing image.
◈ If the pain spread over a larger area the healer used the feminine, receptive, blunter end of the crystal and covered the entire area with exaggerated stroking movements. As the crystal came off the body she flicked it into the air, discarding negative energy.

COUNTERING TRAUMA

Janeen had contracted the HIV virus. She decided to
try crystal healing, having become traumatized and
distanced from loved ones. The healer focused on
Janeen's anger and fearfulness rather than on the virus
itself. She began by creating an atmosphere of love and
serenity, positioning six pieces of rose quartz in a star
shape around her. This produced a positive energy
fused with love and support, projected and amplified
through the crystals.

◆ Hematite, placed alongside the
rose quartz, provided the
grounding that facilitates the
expression of intense emotion
and was chosen to help
transform Janeen's negativity.

◆ Aventurine and rose quartz were
placed over Janeen's heart chakra
and blue-laced agate on the
throat chakra. All are soothing,
gentle stones that promote physical, mental, and emotional well-
being.

Janeen was able to release much
pent-up negative emotion and afterwards felt able to face the future
more positively.

REALIZING POTENTIAL

Jackie had never fully realized her true potential in life.
She felt physically and mentally exhausted, resenting
her present job and wanting a change of career.
However she feared that she was too old to retrain.
Jackie would subconsciously sabotage any efforts she
made by falling ill when she had made an appointment
to discuss a new direction.

Her crystal practitioner selected the following stones
for a full body layout:

◈ Hematite at the base chakra to boost energy and
  vitality, plus a bloodstone to reinforce belief in
  talents.
◈ A single-terminated clear quartz (apex upward)
  to channel energy through the chakras.
◈ A stress-relieving aventurine quartz at her
  "personal power" chakra (the sacral).
◈ At the solar plexus, another piece of citrine for
  optimism and mental clarity.
◈ To boost self-esteem and engender self-love,
  pieces of rose quartz at the heart chakra, plus
  watermelon tourmaline and green nephrite (jade)
  for balance.
◈ At the throat chakra aquamarine, turquoise, and
  blue-laced agate to help self-expression.
◈ On the third eye an amethyst to absorb negativity.
◈ Small, double-terminated pieces of clear quartz
  were positioned between chakras to assist energy
  flow.

Both Jackie and the therapist focused on a positive,
satisfying, and viable outcome for the future.

New technologies

Electro-crystal therapy

This benefits people who simply want more energy, those with medical symptoms ranging from shingles and arthritis to cancer, plus those suffering behavioural problems and stress. The treatment involves a variety of technologies. Before the therapy itself, the body is scanned with a specially adapted video camera that relays a coloured picture of the three-dimensional auric field on to a computer screen. This has been termed "Polycontrast Interface Photography" – or PIP scan.

The coloured PIP scan image (see p.119) may show the patient's bio-electromagnetic field in a disorganized or unbalanced state. The therapist will earmark those areas where the colour of the auric field is inappropriate – such as aggressive, red energy in the head or throat area – indicating stress or a future infection. Essentially, all colours show up in the aura and it is the skill of the therapist that determines which areas require concern and could cause dis-ease if not attended to.

The advantage of the PIP scan is that the patient can receive a print-out of their aura before and after treatment, for comparison. The image can also be stored on computer disk and kept for future reference.

Electro-crystal therapy uses quartz crystals in saline solution that are enclosed in a sealed, glass electrode connected to rechargeable battery packs. Depending on the extent or number of conditions to be treated, up to five electrodes are placed against the affected area or over a chakra point. The crystals are then electrically stimulated with electromagnetic pulses of high frequency until they vibrate and resonate to the desired oscillation.

The electrical current is thought to amplify the healing vibration of the crystals which, in turn, act on the "out of tune" frequency of affected cells. Harmful vibrations within the physical body become modified and the auric field is brought back to a harmonious state.

One treatment lasts up to 45 minutes, during which time the patient remains fully clothed and usually seated.

Kinesiology
This form of muscle testing is often used with crystal cards (see p.113) to determine which colour an individual needs to wear. You can try this by holding your crystal card in one hand with the arm outstretched. Ask another person to then press down on that arm. If you are able to resist the pressure then that is the right colour card for you. If not, and your arm can be pushed down easily, you should try another colour.

CRYSTAL CARDS

These were developed as a result of the NASA space pro-
gramme. Astronauts spending considerable time outside
the Earth's magnetic field were found to suffer a
variety of physiological and psychological disorders on
returning home. To combat this they travelled into space
with a number of pyramid-shaped quartz crystals. These
crystals were electronically charged to vibrate at 7.8Hz,
the frequency which was determined to be the mechanical vibration of the Earth.

The crystal cards sold in New Age stores are made of
thin aluminium shaped like a credit card or triangle, into
which a number of tiny corundum crystals are electro-
chemically etched with hydrochloric acid. The acid
changes the aluminium to a crystalline form while at the
same time producing beneficial negative ions.

The cards are then coated with colour and often
punched with a hole so that they can be worn. The combination of colour and crystal frequencies plus the negative ions emitted from the cards produce a health-giving
frequency that resonates with and harmonizes cellular
activity. Each card has a positive and negative side.
Energy is drawn in from the environment through the
negative side and emitted by the positive side.

COCRYSTO

A cocrysto is a hand-held torch that balances the chakras.
It comprises two parts: a copper holder into which fits a
terminated clear quartz crystal and a battery-operated
torch. Between the torch and the crystal pen are fitted
different-coloured stained glass filters. Light from the
crystal torch filters through the stained glass, directing
colour on to the appropriate chakras. Each of the nine filters is made from glass impregnated with oxides of gold,
silver, and copper, resulting in a selection of synthetic
gemstones such as ruby or sapphire.

This instrument is for experienced crystal healers or
other qualified practitioners only,…(continued on p.116)

STRENGTHENING THE CHAKRAS

It is a good idea to strengthen the chakras as part of your self-healing process. Refer to the chart on pages 68-9, which suggests appropriate crystals for each chakra. If you do not possess the specific crystals recommended in the chart, be guided by the colours indicated, but ultimately follow your intuition.

ROOT OR BASE CHAKRA

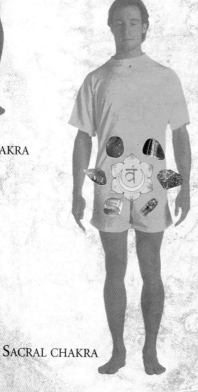

SACRAL CHAKRA

SOLAR PLEXUS CHAKRA

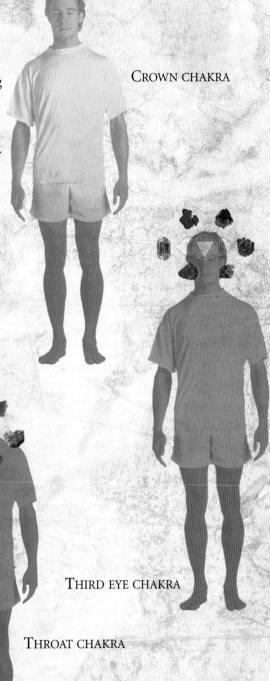

◆ Lie in a comfortable position with your crystals alongside.

◆ Mentally tune in to your inherent healing power.

◆ Become aware of which areas of your body need attention.

◆ Place the crystals singly or in groups over the chakras.

◆ Visualize yourself on a journey (see pp.92-3), achieving your goal of optimum health and wellbeing.

◆ See yourself fit, healthy, and positive. Close the session with the appropriate affirmation (see p.89).

CROWN CHAKRA

THIRD EYE CHAKRA

THROAT CHAKRA

HEART CHAKRA

(continued from p.113) …whose knowledge will determine exactly how the affected chakra should be treated. They will also engage their mind in the process by visualizing the desired outcome.

Patients are advised to dress in white so that the colour from their clothing does not distort the effect from the stained glass filters.

GEM ELIXIRS

A gem elixir is mineral water into which a crystal has been placed and left the memory of its health-giving vibrations. One basic method of producing an elixir is to place a specially tuned crystal into a glass jar or bowl with a quantity of mineral water and to leave it in a special place to absorb the rays of the sun or moon for at least 24 hours. The resulting "energized" water is said to taste sweeter and fresher than the water normally would. To maintain the efficacy of the elixir when stored for any time, mix it with an alcohol such as brandy. Elixirs can be consumed by putting a few drops under the tongue as required.

Any crystal is suitable for producing an elixir, apart from those which are soluble (see p.55). Your choice of crystal will depend on the result you want to achieve (see right). Gem elixirs work on the same principle as homeopathic remedies and flower essences. That homeopathic and Bach Flower remedies have an action is no longer an issue. How they work remains debatable. It is now known that electromagnetic forces are the precursors of chemical reactions. While the chemical molecules of a substance may no longer be present in a dilution, ultra-low frequency resonances remain as a "memory" of its molecular characteristics.

Water is a unique substance with an amazing range of properties – as a gas, liquid, and solid – and tends to be taken for granted. We benefit from its life-giving properties but may also experience it as diseased and deadly. Water is a living substance with an energy cycle of its

Choosing the right gem elixir
Metallic crystals such as hematite and magnetite are useful for grounding. Rose quartz helps promote self-love, and amethyst enhances spirituality and contentment. (For other properties see pp.56-7, 60-1.)

own. One theory suggests that water is in fact a liquid crystal with a double helix structure that stores information in the same way that genetic data is stored in DNA. But regardless of how water manages to retain the template of a substance placed or dissolved to oblivion in it, this electromagnetic imprint continues to resonate with the body's electromagnetic fields and can have a definite effect on it.

ELECTRONIC GEM THERAPY
This therapy brings together the latest technology with traditional Eastern Ayurvedic medicine by combining gem stones, coloured light, and electronic amplification. Conditions treatable using this therapy include asthma, bronchitis, sciatica, psoriasis and eczema, depression, allergies, and lack of energy.

According to Ayurvedic tradition, diseases arising out of too much heat in the body require cooling gems such as carnelian, emerald, and topaz. While those diseases arising from cold within the body, such as low blood pressure, obesity, and constipation need "hot", or warming, gems such as ruby, chrysoberyl, and citrine.

During treatment crystals chosen for their relevant energy output and properties are vibrated electronically. The pulsation rate is set at the particular condition. This gem ray energy is then focused by special coloured lamps, called Gem Transducers, on to whichever area of the body requires treatment. The patient either sits or lies down and can remain fully clothed. Each treatment lasts between 10 and 20 minutes per symptom. Often a single session is enough to give the patient the additional energy needed to bring about self-healing.

EPILOGUE

Some of you may still view crystal healing with scepticism. Others may have embraced it enthusiastically and developed a special relationship with these "flowers of the mineral kingdom". No one therapy can be a panacea for all ills – or all people. Regardless of how you feel about the metaphysics, crystals do have a part to play in your life. Let them grace your home and instil you with a sense of wonder.

Experiment with crystals, have fun with them. Experiment with yourself and the challenging concept that a major capacity for healing lies within YOU.

Emotions have a fundamental part to play in this self-healing process. Laugh at, become angry with, and actively argue about, the ideas presented in this book. By doing so you will help create the environment for change in your current conceptions about health and healing.

Using PIP scans
PIP scans are used by healers to focus on areas of weakness which might benefit from attention. This example (right) shows red on the brow, which indicates mental stress, a propensity to headaches, and a warning of possible eye problems in the future. Red in the throat area also indicates weakness and a tendency to sore throats and other related problems.

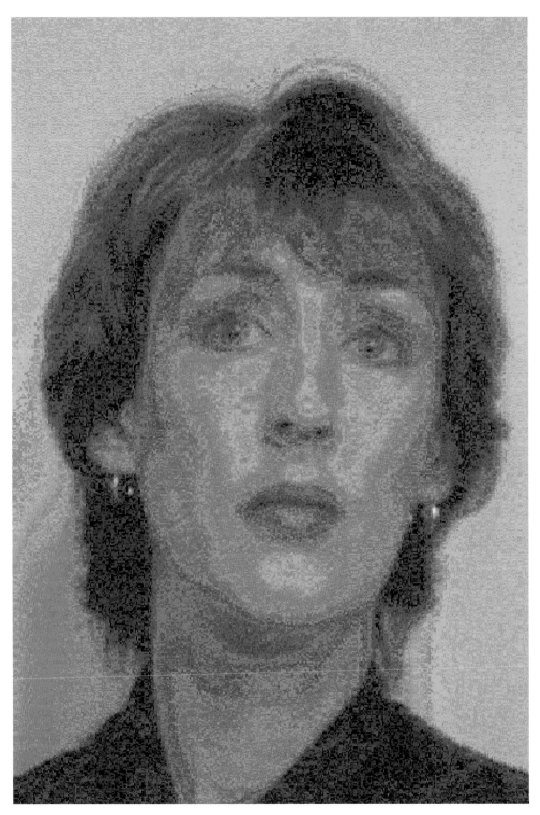

GLOSSARY

AMORPHOUS: Non-crystalline material – without definite internal structure, such as glass.

CLEAVAGE: Where crystals break cleanly along flat planes related to weaknesses in atomic structure.

CRYPTOCRYSTALLINE: Crystals too small to be visible without magnification (e.g. chalcedony group).

CRYSTAL: Solid material with ordered internal atomic structure of regularly repeating three-dimensional patterns. Crystals can be divided into seven groups or systems. Symmetry of atomic structure determines external appearance and physical properties.

CRYSTAL FACES: The flat surfaces of crystals.

CRYSTAL FORM: Geometric shape typical of a particular mineral, which can be classified into one of the seven crystal systems.

CRYSTAL HABIT: External shape of crystals, e.g. needle-like, globular, or prismatic.

CRYSTAL LATTICE: Three-dimensional arrangement of atoms in crystals.

CRYSTALLINE: Material with a crystal structure.

CRYSTALLIZATION: Process which results in formation of crystals.

CRYSTALLOGRAPHY: Scientific study of structure, form, properties of crystals.

CRYSTAL SYSTEMS: The seven groups to which all crystals are classified according to their symmetry: cubic, tetragonal, hexagonal, trigonal, orthorhombic, monoclinic, and triclinic. (Trigonal and hexagonal are one group in USA.)

DISPERSION: Splitting of white light into its seven constituent colours (red, orange, yellow, green, blue, indigo, and violet).

DOUBLE REFRACTION: Splitting of light into two rays, each travelling at different speeds.

FRACTURE: Where crystals break, leaving irregular surface unrelated to atomic structure.

GEMMOLOGY: Scientific study of structure, form, and properties of gems.

GEMSTONE: Decorative material, usually a mineral, considered beautiful, which has clarity of colour or fire and keeps surface polish.

IGNEOUS: Rocks formed from molten magma which may solidify beneath earth's surface or be erupted as lava from volcanoes, e.g. basalt, obsidian, and granite. Crystals found in this type of rock include quartz, olivine, and feldspar.

IMITATION GEMSTONE: Material made to look like a gem which has a different chemical structure and physical properties, e.g. blue glass cut to imitate sapphire.

INCLUSIONS: Solid, liquid, or gas contained in crystal.

LAPIDARY: A craftsman who cuts and polishes gemstones.

LUSTRE: Description of amount of light reflected off surface of a crystal, e.g. vitreous (glass-like) lustre.

MAGMA: Underground, molten rock known as "lava", once erupted.

MASSIVE: Crystals without a definite shape, for instance most rose quartz.

METAMORPHIC: Rock changed from original state by heat and/or pressure into new rock (e.g. marble, schists, and gneisses). May contain garnets, mica, and spinels.

MINERAL: Element or chemical compound naturally formed by geological processes, i.e. inorganic. There are more than 3000 known species of mineral.

PEGMATITE: Slowly cooled igneous rock in which large crystals with complex compositions are formed.

PIEZOELECTRICITY: Property of certain crystals to convert mechanical pressure into electric charge and change electrical energy into precise mechanical vibrations.

PLEOCHROIC: When a crystal appears to have two or more different colours, or shades of colour, depending on viewing angle.

PYROELECTRICITY: Property of some crystals to produce electric charge when heated.

REFRACTION: Bending of light as it passes into a crystal.

REFRACTIVE INDEX (RI): A measure of the degree to

which light rays slow and bend on entering a crystal.

SECONDARY DEPOSITS: Minerals which have been eroded and carried from place of formation and deposited elsewhere. Also known as alluvial or placer deposits.

SEDIMENTARY: Rocks made of sediment from eroded surface rock that has been

carried into river beds or the sea, where it has accumulated and compacted as layers. These include limestone, sandstone, and shale.

SYNTHETIC CRYSTALS: Man-made crystals which have the same composition and properties as their natural counterparts (e.g. quartz in watches and clocks).

RESOURCES

For details of accredited crystal healing organizations offering workshops and full training in crystal healing in the UK, or for their list of crystal healing practitioners, please send A5-sized s.a.e. to:

Affiliation of Crystal Healing Organisations
c/o I.C.C.H.
46 Lower Green Road
Esher
Surrey
KT10 8HD

Crystal Healing Certification Courses in the USA:
Katrina Raphaell
The Crystal Academy of Advanced Healing Arts
PO Box 1334
Kapaa, Hawaii 96746
Tel: (808) 823 6959

Electronic Gem Therapy:
Whale Medical Electronics
Arnside
Cumbria
LA5 0DQ
Tel: 01524 762526

Training and workshops on chakras:
Ruth White
Dragon's Den
3 Manor Farm Lane
Manor Farm Mews
Tidmarsh
Nr. Reading
Berks
RG8 8EY
Tel: 01734 845480

Crystal Cards - Manufacturer:
Micro-Crystal Corporation
PO Box 166
Greenville
Michigan 48838
U.S.A.
Tel: (616) 754 9290

Crystal Cards - UK Supplier:
Gothic Image Limited
7 High Street
Glastonbury
Somerset
BA6 9DP
Tel: 01458 831453

Training in electro-crystal therapy, treatment clinic and details of trained therapists in the UK:
The School of Electro-Crystal Therapy
117 Long Drive
South Ruislip
Middlesex, HA4 0HL
Tel: 0181 841 1716

Cocrysto Colour Crystal Treatment Torch:
Hygeia Manufacturing Limited
Hygeia Studios
Brook House
Avening
Tetbury, Glos. GL8 8NS
Tel: 0145 383 2150

Lecture notes, books, videos, and tapes on Dr Valerie Hunt's work on human energy fields:
Bioenergy Fields Foundation
PO Box 4234
Malibu
California 90265
U.S.A.
Tel: (310) 457 4694

BIBLIOGRAPHY

Allen, John *et al.*, *A Book of Beliefs*, Lion Publishers, 1983

Angelo, Jack, *Your Healing Power*, Piatkus, 1994

Ash, David and Hewitt, Peter, *The Vortex: Key to Future Science*, Gateway Books, 1990

Ash, David, *The New Science of the Spirit*, College of Psychic Studies, 1995

Bunn, Charles, *Crystals – Their Role in Nature and in Science*, Academic Press, 1964

Chopra, Deepak, *Ageless Body, Timeless Mind*, Rider Books, 1993

Collon, Dominique, *Near Eastern Seals*, British Museum Publications, 1990

Dawkins, Richard, *The Blind Watchmaker*, Longmans, 1986

Day, Jennifer, *Creative Visualisation with Children – A Practical Guide*, Element, 1994

Dent, Jennifer, *Crystal Clear: A Guide to the Quartz Crystals*, Capall Bann Publications, 1994

Dent, Jennifer, *Healing Homes*, Capall Bann Publications, 1995

Drexler, K. Eric, *Engines of Creation: The Coming Era of Nanotechnology*, Anchor Books, 1987

Drexler and Peterson with Pergamit, G., *Unbounding the Future: The Nanotechnology Revolution*, William Morrow, 1991

The New Encyclopaedia Britannica, 15th edition, 1987

Fernie, William T., *The Occult and Curative Powers of Precious Stones*, Harper and Row, 1973

Furlong, David, *The Complete Healer*, Piatkus, 1995

Gardner, Joy, *Colors and Crystals: A Journey Through the Chakras*, The Crossing Press, 1988

Gimbel, Theo, *The Book of Colour Healing*, Gaia Books, 1994

Glade, Phyllis, *Crystal Healing – The Next Step*, Llewellyn Publications, 1993

Hackl, Monnica, *Crystal Energy: A Practical Guide to the Use of Crystal Cards for Rejuvenation and Health*, Element, 1994

Hall, Cally, *Identifying Gems and Precious Stones*, The Apple Press, 1993

Hall, Cally, *Gem Stones*, Dorling Kindersley, 1994

Harding, Roger, *Gemstones*, HMSO/Natural History Museum, 1987

Holbeche, Soozi, *The Power of Gems and Crystals*, Piatkus, 1995

Hunt, Valerie V., *Infinite Mind: The Science of Human Vibrations*, Malibu Publishing Co., 1989 and 1995

Hurlbut, Cornelius S., *Minerals and Man*, Thames and Hudson, 1969

Karagulla, Shafica, MD, *The Chakras and The Human Energy Fields*, Quest Books, 1989

Kourimsky, A, *The Illustrated Encyclopedia of Minerals and Rocks*, Sunburst Books, 1995

Kunz, George F., *The Curious Lore of Precious Stones*, Dover Publications, 1971

Kunz, George F., *The Magic of Jewels and Charms*, J.B. Lippincott Co., 1915

Linn, Denise, *Sacred Space: Clearing and Enhancing the Energy of Your Home*, Rider Books, 1995

Melody, *Love in the Earth: A Kaleidoscope of Crystals*, Earth-Love Publishing House, 1995

Mercer, Ian F., *Crystals*, HMSO/Natural History Museum

Molyneaux, Brian Leigh, *The Sacred Earth*, Macmillan, 1995

Muir, Richard, *The Stones of Britain*, Michael Joseph, 1986

O'Donoghue, Michael, *The Pocket Guide to Rocks and Minerals*, Dragon's World, 1990

O'Donoghue, Michael, *Quartz*, Butterworth Gem Books, 1987

O'Kelly, Michael J., *Newgrange – Archaeology, Art and Legend*, Thames and Hudson

Oldfield, Harry and Coghill, Roger, *The Dark Side of the Brain*, Element Books, 1988

Pliny (trans. Eichholz), *Natural History*, Volumes 1 and 10, Loeb Classical Library, Heinemann, 1962

Raphaell, Katrina, *Crystal Enlightenment: The Transforming Properties of Crystals and Healing Stones*, Aurora Press, 1985

Raphaell, Katrina, *Crystal Healing: The Therapeutic Application of Crystals and Stones,* Aurora Press, 1987

Readers Digest, *How Is It Done?* Readers Digest Association, 1990

Robinson, George W. , *Minerals: An Illustrated Exploration of the Dynamic World of Minerals and Their Properties,* Weidenfield and Nicolson, 1994

Roeder, Dorothy, *Crystal Co-Creators,* Light Technology Publishing, 1994

Schumann, W., *Collins Photoguide to Rocks, Minerals and Gemstones,* HarperCollins, 1992

Sheldrake, R., *The Presence of the Past,* HarperCollins, 1994

Silbey, Uma, *The Complete Crystal Guidebook,* Bantam New Age, 1986

Swan, James A., *The Power of Place and Human Environments (An Anthology),* Gateway Books, 1993

Symes, R.F, *Rock and Mineral,* Dorling Kindersley/Natural History Museum, 1988

Symes, R.F. & Harding, Dr. R.R., *Crystal and Gem,* Dorling Kindersley/Natural History Museum, 1991

Tait, Hugh (ed.), *Seven Thousand Years of Jewellery,* British Museum Press, 1986

Taylor, William, *Man andNature,* Regency Press, 1974

Vitebsky, Piers, *The Shaman,* Macmillan, 1995

Walker, Barbara G., *The Book of Sacred Stones: Fact and Fallacy in the Crystal World,* Harper SanFrancisco, 1989

Weil, Andrew, *Spontaneous Healing,* Little, Brown, 1995

White, Ruth, *Working with Your Chakras,* Piatkus, 1993

Zohar, Danah, *The Quantum Self,* Flamingo, 1991

ARTICLES

"Acoustical Resonances of Assorted Ancient Structures", Robert G. Jahn *et al.,* Tech. Report PEAR 95002

Princeton Engineering Anomalies Research, Princeton University, NJ. March 1995

"Evidence for Consciousness-Related Anomalies in Random Physical Systems", Radin & Nelson, Princeton University, 1988

"Out of This Aboriginal Sensible Muchness": Consciousness, Information and Human Health;

Robert G. Jahn, The Journal of the American Society for Psychical Research, Vol. 89, no. 4, Oct. 1995

Article on Sacred Geometry, *Encounters* magazine, Issue 8, June 1996, pp.10-13

"Our Crystal Planet: Is a Broken Web of Power Our Legacy from the Distant Past?", Atlantis Rising Issue 7, 1996, p.20.

"Core of the Earth May Be a Gigantic Crystal Made of Iron", New York Times, Tuesday, April 4, 1995

Video: *Recovering the Soul,* Larry Dossey

Video: *The Human Energy Field & Health with Dr. Valerie V. Hunt,* Bioenergy Fields Foundation, 1993

INDEX

ACKNOWLEDGEMENTS

Author's acknowledgements
My grateful thanks for their advice, encouragement, and allowing me to pick their brains at length go to:
Cathy Oldershaw; Ruth White; the staff at the Minerology department and General Libraries of the Natural History Museum, London; Princeton Engineering Anomalies Research (PEAR) laboratory; Dr Valerie V. Hunt; The Gemmological Association of Great Britain; Helen Carlton and Stephanie Collins of the

International College of Crystal Healing; John Lydon, Senior Lecturer, Department of Biochemistry and Molecular Biology, Leeds University, UK; David Lorimer, The Scientific and Medical Network, UK; Christopher Portman; Caroline Hedicker; Nigel Israel; David A. Ash; Harry Oldfield; Katrina Raphaell; and the many owners of websites on the Internet whose generosity in making information freely available helped to put me on the right track. Special thanks also to Jo

Godfrey Wood, Sara Mathews, and Pip Morgan of Gaia Books for being such a pleasure to work with.

Publisher's acknowledgements
Gaia Books would like to thank Robert Burns, Phil Gamble, Patrick Furse (design assistance), Lynn Bresler (index), Richard Philpot (picture research), Mike Dean.

Other books in the series

Healing with Colour
Theo Gimbel
£10.99
ISBN 1 85675 026 4
A practical guide to using colour in clothes, interior design and treatments to improve your health and vitality.

Healing with Sound
Olivea Dewhurst-Maddock
£10.99
ISBN 1 85675 023 X
A new edition of this authoritative introduction to the healing energies of sound, featuring the range of practical techniques used in sound therapy.

More titles from Gaia Books

The Healing Power of Sleep
How to achieve restorative sleep naturally
Sheila Lavery
£11.99
ISBN 1 85675 0086
A practical self-help guide to improve personal sleeping habits and the quality of our sleep by understanding what happens while we sleep and why sleep is important to our health.

Aromatherapy for Healing the Spirit
A guide to restoring emotional and mental balance through essential oils
Gabriel Mojay
£10.99
ISBN 1 85675 072 8
Individual treatments for a range of psychological problems, from anxiety to stress.

Step-by-Step Tui Na
Maria Mercati
£14.99 H/B
ISBN 1 85675 038 8
This clear step-by-step guide introduces Tui Na, a healing system of energising massage and manipulation from Traditional Chinese Medicine.
Now available in paperback
£11.99 P/B
ISBN 1 85675 044 2

Massage for Pain Relief
Peijian Shen
£10.99
ISBN 1 85675 052 3
Clear, authoritative text and detailed illustrations demonstrate self-healing massage techniques as well as how to treat others.

For a catalogue of titles published by Gaia Books, write or phone Gaia Books, 20 High Street, Stroud, Gloucestershire GL5 1AS.
Tel: 01453 752985 Fax: 01453 752987 e-mail: Gaiabook@star.co.uk